THE LIBERATION OF EUROPE

THE LIBERATION OF EUROPE

The Photographers who Captured History from D-Day to Berlin

Mark Barnes

CASEMATE
Oxford & Philadelphia

Published in Great Britain and
the United States of America in 2016 by
CASEMATE PUBLISHERS
10 Hythe Bridge Street, Oxford OX1 2EW, UK
and
1950 Lawrence Road, Havertown PA 19083, USA

Hardcover Edition: ISBN 978-1-61200-402-0
Digital Edition: ISBN 978-1-61200-406-8
A CIP record for this book is available from the British Library

Typeset in the UK by Frabjous Books
Printed and bound in the Czech Republic by FINIDR

For a complete list of Casemate titles, please contact:
CASEMATE PUBLISHERS (UK)
Telephone (01865) 241249
Fax (01865) 794449
Email: casemate-uk@casematepublishers.co.uk
www.casematepublishers.co.uk

CASEMATE PUBLISHERS (US)
Telephone (610) 853-9131
Fax (610) 853-9146
Email: casemate@casematepublishers.com
www.casematepublishers.com

TITLE PAGE Bill Warhurst strikes a typical pose for the camera during Operation *Veritable*. The cigarette holder was a near-permanent fixture. A veteran staff photographer for *The Times,* he enjoyed a prolific career including coverage of the discovery of Tutankhamun's tomb, the Abyssinian War and the series of events from the Munich crisis onwards that led him to be standing on a muddy track in the Reichswald Forest in February 1945.
Herbert W. Warhurst, The Times WN6364

ABOVE At the height of the Normandy campaign Bill Warhurst spent time at a leave camp where he photographed a number of men, including (left to right): Sergeant W. Haywood from Barking, Driver W. Ellis from Lincoln, Signaller G. P. Ditchburn from Swansea, Gunner G. Philpotts from Pontypridd, Private E. Hunter from Bradford and Trooper Dennis Dolby from Birmingham.
Herbert W. Warhurst, The Times WN5095a, WN5086, WN5088, WN5091, WN5104, WN5085

CONTENTS

ACKNOWLEDGEMENTS

———————

I am immensely grateful to the following for helping to make this book happen – John Baker, Adrian Barrell, Jack Beckett, Ray Bradbury, Dean Burrows, Matt Buston, Stephen Carr, Mike Haines, Phil Hodges, Steve Hood, Nigel Julian, Simon Last, Mike Lawn, Roger Morris, Joris Nieuwint, Wayne Osborne, Anthony Sewards, Simon Thomson, John Trafford and Paul Woodage. I'd especially like to thank Winston Ramsey for all his inspiration and encouragement.

Clare Litt and Ruth Sheppard at Casemate UK and Martin Gibbs at News Syndication have been instrumental in getting the book into print. Thank you for helping make a dream come true.

At News UK I must thank Robin Ashton, Steve Baker, Anne Jensen, Nick Mays, Steve Nicoll, Andrew Sims and Chris Whalley. Thanks also to my fellow content specialists for their support – Chris Ball, Mark Brown, Lee Chilvers, Sue De Friend, Richard Hodson, Michael-John Jennings, Robert Newsome and Marc Russell.

Geoff Baker, James Baker, Phil Cunningham, Stephen Firminger, Lance Flower, Mark Flower, Rob Lawrence, Chris Levell, Ted Meadows and Steve Robinson were always on hand with another fiver for the whip.

Last but not least, I must pay tribute to my son and daughter James and Emily Barnes, for being there during the highs and lows. I couldn't have done it without you.

INTRODUCTION

The first thoughts of doing this book occurred back in 2000 when I matched images taken by Bill Warhurst and Bill Tetlow during the assault on Münster. I thought it was pretty cool but I have long appreciated my military history interests set me apart from the many librarians I have worked with. I was sure bringing the images together would make a great book. There were, however, other priorities; especially during the period when digitisation was sweeping away traditional library practices. But it was this very process that made this book possible. Having the means to digitally scan the original negatives was the clincher and I am grateful to my managers for seeing merit in what I wanted to achieve.

Getting all the images together was not always straightforward. *The Times* had a penchant for making special negative diaries for notable events, so the material by Eric Greenwood, Cathal O'Gorman and Bill Warhurst was kept together. Very few of the original negatives that arrived at Printing House Square are missing and the scanning process allowed me to re-file one or two that were in the wrong order. With the Kemsley material it was a different matter. The collection had gone through a deletion process during the early 1970s and a good many negatives are lost. Although a 'Pool negs' diary was started in 1944, it was written up in no particular order and it is apparent that the wartime librarians were casual with their methodology. The diary lists around a dozen blocks of negatives with separate reference numbers, but when additional batches were received the librarians recorded them in the day-to-day diary, instead, and no effort was made at cross-referencing.

Further complications occurred in 1952 when a number of Kemsley's Pool negatives were removed for printing. Rather than re-file them the whole lot were given new numbers in a sequence of references begun after the Second World War. This was compounded by the fact the traditional method of writing the negative number in the plate's margin with a fountain pen or the point of a compass had been largely discontinued as glass plates increasingly gave

TOP A few of Eric Greenwood's 120 roll film negatives taken with his 'special light camera' on D-Day. The model he used is not known. Some of Greenwood's films were fogged during processing back in London. Another hazard was the loss of films altogether. Both Greenwood and Warhurst have missing frames noted in the campaign 'neg diaries'. Damaged cameras could also be a problem and Frederick Skinner of Kemsley was certainly a victim during 1945 but he soldiered on with what he had.

Author

RIGHT A carbon copy of one of Eric Greenwood's caption sheets from D-Day. This one relates to the period around 1030hrs and mentions Admiral Talbot's command ship HMS *Largs* and the landings on Juno Beach. The top sheet plus carbon copies were wrapped up with the exposed film and delivered to London for processing. Photographers provided notes to complete the typed-up captions accompanying the image for censoring and any subsequent use. Some wrote detailed captions themselves but there are examples where the correct spelling of place names and such like was an issue. Although the censor would usually delete names of individuals and units for publication purposes, the sporadic inclusion of these details is a great help to librarians. This carbon found its way to the picture library at Printing House Square where it added to information written up in the 'day book' or 'neg diary'. Caption sheets like this were usually thrown away afterwards, so this is a rare survivor. Some of the notes made by Kemsley photographers were extensive and have proven essential with preparing this book.

Content Operations – News UK

TOP This image shows two pages from the negatives diary listing Eric Greenwood's work on D-Day. This sequence is for films taken on board HMS *Scylla* off Sword Beach at around 0730hrs on D-Day. A librarian wrote up the book using the captions and notes sent by the photographer.

Author

LEFT There is much less to see from this entry for Bill Warhurst's coverage of the suicide of Heinrich Himmler in May 1945. Listings from the last days of Warhurst's time in Germany betray a degree of fatigue with the whole experience. Hardly surprising given the pace of events and the conditions he was working under.

Author

FOR IMMEDIATE PUBLICATION.
BRITISH NEWSPAPER POOL PHOTOGRAPH. NO. 383761
DISTRIBUTED BY P.N.A. 30 FLEET STREET.
TELEPHONE CENTRAL 8982.
PHOTO BY SKINNER-DAILY SKETCH.

FUNERAL OF ADMIRAL RAMSEY.

Photo shows: Chief mourners at the graveside.
Left to right. Gen. Koenig, Admiral Cunningham,
Gen. Eisenhower. and Mr. Duff Cooper.

9/1/45   P.N.A. 30 FLEET STREET. E.C.4.

TOP A page from the Kemsley Newspapers Pool negatives diary. The random order of entries indicates that the diary was made retrospectively without strong attention to keeping the listings in date order. The column on the left is for British Newspaper Pool reference numbers.

Author

LEFT A typical Kemsley Newspapers negative packet with British Newspaper Pool caption label and Pool and filing reference numbers. An image from Admiral Bertram Ramsay's funeral is shown on page 157.

Author

way to film. Fortunately the Pool negatives filed in 1944/45 included many that had their numbers or were, at least, easy to match to a specific packet.

The other element was the prints. With a fair number of negatives missing, they became even more valuable with the loss of the 'first generation' image. Fortunately, the Kemsley print collection is full of them. *The Times* and Kemsley prints from the campaign offer a mine of information from the physical elements of the images themselves to details about censorship, the Pool numbering system, filing references and publication dates. The standards of film processing during 1944/45 were occasionally haphazard and some negatives have deteriorated because they were not fixed adequately or suffer from oxidisation. Having a print, often in near new condition, is a huge bonus.

The British Newspaper Pool ran from just before D-Day to around the time of the Potsdam conference. The high command could not accommodate an army of photographers gambolling about the front line, so sharing images was the most practical way to meet demand. The Pool's output joined the material from official sources and news agencies vying for space with images from US providers. Not all national newspapers participated but a number of regional titles such as the *Yorkshire Post*, did. Their photographer Herbert Dewhirst took some outstanding images. The workings of the Pool explain how some of the most well-known images from this book can be found in the collections of a number of sources today including the Imperial War Museum, which has many on file. *The Times* and Kemsley were separate companies but one success of the Pool after all this time was finding missing Kemsley images filed as prints in *The Times* system. This shows the enduring value of an arrangement made over seventy years ago. The use of pools or 'rotas', as they are often known, continue to this day; usually for official occasions involving the royal family.

Compiling this book has been a joy but the real difficulty came with deciding what to leave out. There are so many fascinating images but a good deal of the original plan for this book ended up on the cutting room floor. Including any more images than are here already would present more to look at but would not necessarily add anything significant to the story of the campaign.

I went to school in Hackney and on a field trip forty-two years ago my French teacher, Mr Jackson, told me how he had crossed the Rhine by tank in 1945. This book is for all the Mr Jacksons of the North-West Europe campaign. Old soldiers never die; they only fade away.

Mark Barnes
January 2016

TOP This Van Neck VNB99 Press Camera is typical of the plate cameras used before film formats dominated the industry after the Second World War. This particular camera dates from just after the war but the basis of the design, size and weight is the same as cameras used by the men featured in this book. Dennis Risley, the son of the pioneering Edward, who took the war memorial image shown at the beginning of this book, used the camera when he worked for *The Times* during the 1950s. By coincidence, Bill Warhurst's son Gerrard, also known as Bill, was a photographer for the paper.

Author

BOTTOM German cameras were much imitated but rarely bettered by foreign competitors until Japanese firms dominated the post-war market. Leica's 35mm cameras were especially admired and it was inevitable they would be copied. The Candid Camera Corporation of Chicago made the 1939 vintage Perfex Forty-Four on the left and it sold reasonably well. The manufacturers got round patents by changing key features such as the focusing ring. It is at the back of the lens and somewhat counter intuitive to usual experience. This was just one of a number of modifications implemented to get this fiddly camera into production. At the end of the war the Allies made all German patents public, making copying easier. Large numbers were made in the Soviet Union and this FED 2 is typical of a range that saw over eight million produced between 1946 and 1968.

Author

CHANGING TIMES

At 3.15 in the afternoon of 22nd November 1921 Douglas Haig unveiled the memorial to over sixty employees of *The Times* who had died during the Great War. He told the assembly gathered at Printing House Square 'Victory in war is a barren and unprofitable thing if we cannot reap the fruits of it in peace.' The day heralded an exciting period that would see *The Times* enjoy a rich harvest from having a front-row seat at some of the most memorable events of the 20th century. The discovery of Tutankhamun and the first flight over Everest punctuated dramatic episodes of political upheaval, financial depression and constitutional crisis. As the years passed divisions over how to deal with Hitler and Mussolini were scarcely off the agenda. Events in Abyssinia and Spain signalled things to come and the paper was on hand to record it all. But the biggest story of the century would come when Britain was plunged into another world war less than two decades after that grey Wednesday in the City of London.

The year 1921 was auspicious because *The Times* had somewhat belatedly embraced photography and by the time of the unveiling ceremony Edward Risley, the paper's first full-time photographer, was on hand to record the solemn scene. Risley was both innovative and fearless. His determination to get a picture would soon find him on the wrong side of the law but he stood his ground and set high standards. Along with contemporaries such as James Jarché he was a leader in the consistently dynamic field of news photography as it progressed in the years after the Great War.

The company soon employed a second photographer; the exceptional Herbert William Warhurst, a south Londoner whose father had managed a photo agency. Forever known as Bill, Warhurst photographed significant people and events

from the Valley of the Kings to Lüneburg Heath. Like most press photographers of the period, he was technically skilled and able to make the most of a broad range of subjects. He had an affinity with all things naval but often took the chance to photograph the rural scenes the establishment readership of the paper admired.

Warhurst made for an imposing figure; he was a big man usually seen working with a trademark cigarette holder clenched between his teeth. Much travelled, he fits perfectly into our image of the archetypal Englishman abroad using his physical presence and a natural ebullience to steamroller a path through problems with languages and local proclivities to get what he wanted. The wartime campaign in North-West Europe would give Bill Warhurst the action he craved and he would not waste the opportunity.

Edward Risley died young but he had pioneered photography in a newspaper that was traditionalist and yet innovative with continuous experiments in photographic processes under the watchful eyes of art editor Ulric van den Bogaerde. The stable of photographers would expand to include men keen to try colour processes or indulge in the craze for aerial photography. They made it all work and the results speak for themselves.

The majority share holding in *The Times* had been acquired by John Jacob Astor V in 1922 after the death of Lord Northcliffe. The driving force behind the paper was John Walter (the fourth), the great-great grandson of his namesake who founded the paper in 1785. Born in 1873, he inherited his role in the business in 1910 after a period of great difficulty for the firm and he enjoyed a challenging relationship with Northcliffe, who saw himself as the moneyman, telling Walter 'Your people made it and you have a son to inherit it. I am only here to put it on its legs again.' If ever there was a man with ink in his veins it was John Walter who did not retire until 1960 and stayed involved with the company until it was bought by Roy Thomson six years later. He died in 1968 aged 95.

John Jacob Astor was born in New York City in 1886 and came to England with his father William Waldorf Astor at the age of five. The elder Astor took British citizenship and was raised to the peerage during the Great War. The Astor family lived a quintessentially privileged English lifestyle at Cliveden and following his education at Eton and New College Oxford Astor became a professional soldier with the Life Guards. A keen sportsman, he won gold and bronze medals at racquets for Great Britain at the 1908 London Olympics. Astor served with distinction during the Great War and rose to the rank of lieutenant colonel. Having recovered from wounds received at Messines in 1914 he commanded the 520th (Household) Siege Battery of the Royal Garrison Artillery but he was seriously wounded at Cambrai in September 1918 and lost a leg, ending his army career. Despite his injury he retained strong military connections after the war holding honorary colonelcies in the Royal Artillery and the London Regiment. He commanded a Home Guard battalion predominantly made up from newspaper workers during the Second World War. John Jacob Astor was, in many respects, an ideal proprietor. He rarely involved himself in editorial matters and his 'hands off' approach left the politics to John Walter and his editorial staff.

Across the Square Mile from Queen Victoria Street, Allied Newspapers was home to a group of titles under the control of a proprietor who was the embodiment of a press baron. Born in 1883, Lord Kemsley - James Gomer Berry – was the third son of a Merthyr Tydfil solicitor and estate agent. Along with his two older brothers he was a successful entrepreneur and had chosen journalism as his profession. Working with his brother William, the similarly ennobled Lord Camrose, he used profits from coal interests to build a publishing empire in partnership with Lord Iliffe. Their company acquired *The Sunday Times* in 1915, the *Daily Record* in 1922 and the *Daily Sketch* in 1925.

Allied bought the *Daily Telegraph* in 1927 and continued to grow with a succession of acquisitions. Ten years later the three press magnates broke up their business with Lord Camrose taking the *Telegraph* and the Amalgamated Press group. Lord Kemsley asserted his independence and named his new company and offices after himself. The Kemsley Newspapers stable expanded again, in 1939, when the now largely forgotten *Sunday Referee* was added to the inventory although it was quickly merged with another long-lost title, the *Sunday Chronicle*. Kemsley

had grown to be the largest newspaper group in the United Kingdom publishing national titles from London, Glasgow and Manchester and regional papers in Newcastle and elsewhere.

Lord Kemsley was particularly devoted to *The Sunday Times* and in the twin roles of editor-in-chief and proprietor he was living the dream enjoying his status as an influential press baron who had the ear of powerful men. Although *The Sunday Times* afforded him prestige, Kemsley understood the value of the *Daily Sketch*. The paper was populist and pro-Conservative in outlook, and appealed to the aspirations of the man in the street. It maintained a wary eye on the rise of fascism and from its position on the centre right it supported Neville Chamberlain's pursuit of appeasement.

Over at Printing House Square *The Times* advocated appeasement under editor Geoffrey Dawson who would not publish criticism of Hitler's regime for fear of undermining Neville Chamberlain. Ironically, Nazi hostility to the paper was palpable and Joseph Goebbels' propagandists delighted in taking swipes at what they saw as a cheerleader of the so-called 'international Jewish conspiracy'. The Nazis mocking of *The Times* and frequent seizure of editions came as the paper sat squarely behind Chamberlain while he negotiated with Adolf Hitler. In September 1938 Bill Warhurst travelled to Bad Godesberg to photograph the summit that gave no succour to a beleaguered Czechoslovakia and managed to get a couple of plates showing the two men standing stiffly in the charged atmosphere. It is said he stood alone in a room with Hitler for several awkward minutes waiting for Chamberlain to arrive. With the stark failure of appeasement both Astor and Lord Kemsley would place their papers firmly behind the war effort against the Axis powers.

At the start of the Second World War *The Times* boasted a first-class team of photographers who could turn their hand to pretty much anything the paper required. As with many facets of the newspaper industry, photography was seen as a respectable trade and exponents of it had typically spent their formative years in the industry working in dark rooms. Sound knowledge of materials, processing and printing and many of the black arts attached to them were essential in an age when the instant photography we know today was unheard of.

Staff man Cathal O'Gorman was a gifted aerial photographer while Eric Greenwood had successfully photographed royalty using colour film. Both men were skilled all-rounders like Bill Warhurst with their own specialisms.

Over at Kemsley the in-house photographer pool worked for all titles in the group but the lion's share of images appeared in the *Daily Sketch* where the editorial team perfected a powerful and graphic use of photography that lives on in the modern-day popular press.

Although a range of film cameras from Eastman Kodak and others had popularised photography for the general user, the vast majority of press imagery from the first half of the century was made using photographic plates, a process whereby light-sensitive emulsion was coated on thin glass. Although appreciated for their image quality, glass plates presented all manner of problems for both carriage and storage that continue to impact on photographic collections to this day. The picture library at Printing House Square grew steadily in the hands of the redoubtable Maude Davies who learned as she went, eventually settling on a simple linear numbering system for each plate. The Kemsley picture library had changed hands several times but by the start of the Second World War an alphanumeric system was long since established. Strict adherence to it proved to be confusing, to say the least, and the results present a challenge to the librarians using it today.

Despite the eventual domination of film, glass plates remained common in newspaper use well into the 1960s and some papers were still using them for making copy negatives in the late 1970s. Although press cameras of the period were heavy they were considered robust and required practice enabling users to identify themselves as the skilful professionals they undoubtedly were. Photographers were restricted by the number of plates they could carry and limited by the speed they could change plates as they worked but this does not appear to have held them back to any degree.

A key player in the British press camera market was Peeling & Van Neck based at their premises in Holborn, an address conveniently close to Fleet Street. Aside from cameras the company produced a range of photography essentials. Their efforts to manufacture colour transparency film were endorsed by *The Times*, whose experiments with Autochrome had yielded images for special colour supplements before the war and despite intense demands on British manufacturing during the war Peeling & Van Neck were able to introduce an improved press camera in 1943.

It was during this period that Herbert William Tetlow joined Kemsley. He enjoyed a long career in news photography working for several agencies including the Associated Press and Fox Photos. Like Bill Warhurst he did not use his first name. Inspiration for this book came from discovering moments when the two Bills came together during the North-West Europe campaign recording events in different styles for their respective newspapers.

While the many members of the press soldiered on with the likes of the Van Neck the advancement in medium format and 35mm film cameras revolutionised photography. Practically any German film cameras were highly prized and although they were much imitated, notably by inferior American copies such as the Perfex Forty-Four; it was the Leica that was most sought after. Kemsley men were sporadic users of Leicas before the war but there was never any doubt that the use of 35mm film stock would be minimal in comparison to the dependency on glass plate. As we shall see, other film formats were used on occasion and Bill Tetlow used a range of them to record events in post-war Berlin.

Throughout the Second World War Kemsley's team of photographers took in excess of 11,000 images a year while those of *The Times* managed 17,000 for the entire conflict. A typical edition of the paper would carry no more than six or seven images with the majority appearing on its 'picture page'. Things were very different over at Kemsley House where the conflict inspired the use of bold imagery rather than inhibited it.

The war would present a range of huge challenges to press photography both in terms of its execution and getting the results in print. Neither *The Times* nor Kemsley Newspapers sent photographers to cover the campaigns in North Africa, Italy or Asia. Although the papers sent correspondents to the other theatres, receiving images from staff photographers was a logistical headache with attendant cost implications that were just not worth meeting. Wire images could be transmitted by telephone line, but the fluid situations of campaigns in far-off places with poor communications made reliance on official and agency material much more practical. In consequence, they found themselves more or less confined to events at home until the British Newspaper Pool was established to share images of the invasion of France in 1944. Getting images back from the Continent was achieved by access to couriers travelling to and from Britain.

On 13th May 1940, three days after the start of the German Blitzkrieg in the west, Winston Churchill stood up in Parliament and made his famous speech of defiance after the bitter end to Neville Chamberlain's premiership. 'You ask: "What is our aim?" I can answer in one word: It is victory, victory at all costs, victory in spite of all terror, victory however hard the road may be; for without victory there is no survival.' The first years of Churchill's premiership were, without doubt, all about survival because there were very few meaningful victories and too many humiliations. But success in the desert against the Italians would see many veterans of those early battles absorbed into the Eighth Army by 1942. The Desert Rats and other units from the North African campaign who fought against Rommel in Egypt and Libya would meet him on another day in Normandy in 1944.

As the war progressed *The Times* and Kemsley photographers busied themselves depicting the effects of German bombing, anxious to show how people carried on with their daily lives in spite of the perils. The London offices of both companies were bombed in September 1940 causing severe damage but newspaper production continued. The destruction at Printing House Square came without loss of life even though three hundred staff were in the building at the time. Precautions taken before the war had paid off and the next morning's edition was printed regardless of the mess. Winston Churchill wrote to Astor to congratulate his staff and the next edition of the in-house journal gave a graphic description of events and delighted in adding that twenty years' worth of winning prints from competitions held by the Camera Club were undamaged and 'Like their originators and custodians, refused to bow to Hitler.' Kemsley House was bombed again in the spring of 1944, killing three staff, two of them on Home Guard duty.

The gradual build-up of forces in Britain, in addition to the huge industrial effort was an attractive subject for newspapers. For the *Daily Sketch*, especially, its connection with ordinary people was exploited to show how everyone was working towards a common goal. The arrival of the Americans in early 1942 was of particular interest and as the 'friendly invasion', Operation *Bolero,* expanded there was plenty of scope to record events at US bomber bases and other locations. The steady flow of Hollywood stars and other celebrities in uniform were a constant draw. Meanwhile, room was found at Printing House Square to provide printing facilities for *Stars and Stripes*, the US forces newspaper.

Reporting the bombing offensive against the Reich became the principal way of showing how the Allies were hitting back at Germany and the campaign received plenty of press attention.

There were few qualms about the pounding of German cities at that time. But as time passed the clamour for the 'second front' grew. The return of the victorious General Bernard Law Montgomery to Britain and the arrival of Dwight D Eisenhower to lead the invasion of Europe were noted, but as the year 1944 progressed, secrecy surrounding the readiness of Allied forces was rigorously maintained. Only occasional glimpses of arsenals and weaponry made it into print. Censorship had been strict from the earliest days of the war and occasionally baffling requirements to drastically alter or 'kill' photographs altogether reveal a fascinating aspect of how the conflict was presented to the British public. The campaign in Europe from D-Day onwards would prove just as challenging for the media. Another kind of censorship came in the form of what the public would accept from news photography. Unlike the Great War, images of dead and wounded Allied soldiers were carefully controlled and the faces of British dead never appeared. As we shall see, even the features of wounded men would be obscured from time to time, although visits to hospitals would show plenty of stoic cheeriness and stiff upper lip. Press photographers quickly learned what they could record and generally avoided subjects that would never be used. There would be extreme examples of a reverse to this policy, notably when the British liberated Bergen-Belsen in April 1945.

Four years after Churchill's demand for victory at all costs, Eisenhower's 'Great Crusade' was about to begin. The original intention for this book was to bring together the work of two photographers from the campaign. But just as Clausewitz cautioned that no plan survives first contact, things were not that simple. While the work of Bill Warhurst and Bill Tetlow remains central to the story, four more men became increasingly important. Although we will see the work of others from time to time it is the photography of Bill Warhurst and his colleagues Eric Greenwood and Cathal O'Gorman from *The Times* and Bill Tetlow, R. H. Clough and Frederick Skinner of Kemsley Newspapers who provide the majority of images selected here.

TOP The unveiling ceremony of *The Times* war memorial at Printing House Square as pictured by Edward Risley, 22nd January 1921.

Edward Risley, The Times

BOTTOM Bill Warhurst's photograph of the scene at Bad Godesberg on 23rd September 1938 when Neville Chamberlain arrived to negotiate with Adolf Hitler over the future of Czechoslovakia. Warhurst spent a few silent minutes alone in the room with Hitler before Chamberlain entered.

Herbert W. Warhurst, The Times 77907

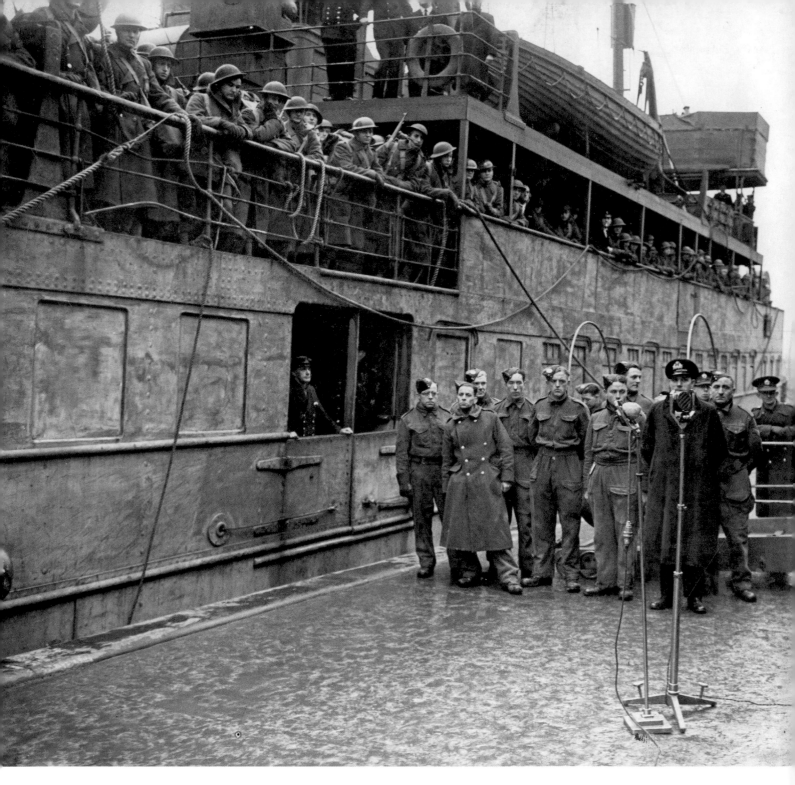

LEFT It could be argued that this somewhat dreary scene photographed by Bill Warhurst is where the beginning of the end of the Nazi regime occurred. The first contingent of US combat troops to arrive in the UK are welcomed by Sir Archibald Sinclair at Dufferin Quay, Belfast on 27th January 1942. The men of the 133rd Infantry Regiment heard the Secretary of State for Air tell them 'From here assuredly you will sally forth with us to carry war into the enemy's territory and free the oppressed peoples of Europe.... Your arrival marks a new stage in the world war.' 26th January 1942.

Herbert W. Warhurst, The Times 94083

TOP RIGHT *The Times'* aerial photography specialist Cathal O'Gorman found plenty to keep him busy when he was taken up to photograph Republic P-47C Thunderbolts of the 56th Fighter Group flying from RAF Kings Cliffe on 10th April 1943. The three squadrons of the 56th were working up to combat readiness at their Northamptonshire base. On this same day the 4th Fighter Group became operational and the media visit to Kings Cliffe was timed to correspond with their first combat mission over occupied Europe.

Cathal O'Gorman, The Times 96936A

BOTTOM RIGHT Lieutenant-General Omar N. Bradley pictured with Brigadier-General William B. Kean in London on 7th January 1944. This image was 'killed' by the censor, with special reference made to not show Kean, Bradley's Chief of Staff, who went on to be promoted to major-general and become Chief of Staff of the US First Army.

Robert Chandler, Kemsley M4232T

TOP The invasion chiefs gather for their introduction to the media at Norfolk House on 1st February 1944. Eisenhower and Monty are deep in conversation while Arthur Tedder looks bored with it all. Omar N. Bradley, Bertram Ramsay, Trafford Leigh-Mallory and Walter Bedell Smith stand at the back.

Herbert W. Warhurst, The Times 98770

BOTTOM The gathering of 'invasion chiefs' in London was the cause of some interest, not least the appearance of General Bernard Law Montgomery fresh from campaigning in Italy and now ground forces commander for *Overlord*. Monty gives a quick wave to his many admirers gathered outside Norfolk House on 21st April 1944.

Robert Chandler, Kemsley M4233K

TOP Although expectation for the Second Front was high, only a relatively small number of images of the build-up of men and weapons for the invasion of France were published in newspapers. This view of new BL 5.5 inch medium guns amassed at the Chilwell Ordnance Depot in Nottingham appeared on 27th April 1944.

H. William Tetlow, Kemsley M4238W

BOTTOM Preparations for the invasion were not all about weapons. This image shows an impressive display of *Golden Arrow* signals vehicles and their generators. Named after the well-known train service, each self-contained unit comprised Bedford OXC sending and receiving tractor-trailer units, two Bedord QL 3 ton trucks to tow generators and a 1500 cwt Tilly for the commanding officer. A complement of 22 men, including a cook, manned these units that were used for high-level communications including Ultra signals. Some *Golden Arrows* also transmitted press reports back to Britain. The sending and receiving trailers and aerial arrays were ideally set up 400 yards apart to reduce interference. The signallers manning the equipment were an elite, chosen for their high skill levels.

Albert Abrahams, Kemsley M4236G

The art of the 'join-up' – the practice of making a wide image from two others – was standard stuff for most newspapers. The judicious use of a pin board is typical of the methodology. Others, minus the pins, will be seen later. The finished version of this image appeared under the headline 'Arms That Await the Hour' on 27th April 1944, but a cursory glance reveals little of the weaponry that would take part in the invasion in clear view. The Canadian Ram tank on the left was never used in combat in the form shown and the Crusader tank in the foreground was already obsolete. The Cromwell tank on the right would see sterling service in the North-West Europe campaign.

H. William Tetlow, Kemsley M4238W

LEFT The use of montages, the art of overlaying multiple images to make up one, was tricky but the impact was generally impressive and modern-day newspapers are still keen on them. This image of an 8th Air Force Boeing B-17 Flying Fortress returning from a raid with the bombers overhead coming from one or more other negatives was published under the headline 'Towards the Twilight of the Luftwaffe' on 13th April 1944. The original negatives of the various elements do not survive.

Kemsley M4238B

TOP RIGHT Before D-Day, attacks on German armour concentrations were a top priority. On the night of 3rd/4th May 1944 a force of 346 Lancasters supported by Mosquitoes attacked the home base of 21st Panzer Division at Mailly-le-Camp. It was an expensive raid with 42 Lancasters lost. One of the aircraft taking part was Avro Lancaster B.Mk.1 R5868 'S-Sugar' of 467 Squadron RAAF from RAF Waddington on its ninety-ninth bombing sortie. Captained by Pilot Officer Tom Scholefield of Cryon, Australia, the Lancaster dropped a 4,000lb 'Cookie' and sixteen 500lb bombs on the target during a five and a half hour round trip. Scholefield was quoted in the Australian media saying 'The depot looked like an inferno. I saw my stick of bombs land on the target. I have never seen what my bombs hit so clearly before, not even on practice bombing. There were a lot of fighters about, but they did not interfere with our bombing run.' The raiders dropped 1,500 tons of bombs on the panzer division's depot. The crew of 'S for Sugar' posed for the press reporting the aircraft's '97th' raid. Left to right: Pilot Officer T. N. Scholefield; Flying Officer I. Hamilton of Coatbridge, Lanarkshire; Flt Sergeant F. R. T. Hillas of Victoria, Australia; Flt Sergeant F. E. Hughes of Melbourne, Australia; Sergeant R. H. Burgess of Cheshire; Flt Sergeant K. E. Stewart of Sydney, Australia and Sergeant J. D. Wells of Sidcup, Kent.

Robert Chandler, Kemsley M4239J

BOTTOM RIGHT Armourers and fitters prepare 'S-Sugar' ahead of her trip to Mailly-le-Camp. This aircraft completed a remarkable 140 sorties and was retained for preservation after the war. It can be seen at the RAF Museum Hendon.

Robert Chandler, Kemsley M4239J

THE LIBERATION OF EUROPE 1944–1945

This striking image by Robert Chandler shows pilots of No 485 Squadron RNZAF attending an open-air briefing on 27th May 1944. This squadron were just one of many engaged in attacking ground targets ahead of D-Day and this image appeared in print under the headline 'RAF Loco busters' reflecting the devastation of French and Belgian railways carried out by the Allied air forces to interdict the movement of German forces.

Robert Chandler, Kemsley M4241B

An artist produced this impression of what D-Day would look like for the *Daily Sketch*. Although it is more akin to the imagery of British comics of the 1950s and 1960s it is interesting to compare this scene with actual events.

Kemsley M4239S

OVERLORD

Soldiers, Sailors and Airmen of the Allied Expeditionary Force!
You are about to embark upon the Great Crusade, toward which we have striven these many months. The eyes of
the world are upon you. The hopes and prayers of liberty-loving people everywhere march with you. In company
with our brave Allies and brothers-in-arms on other Fronts, you will bring about the destruction of the German
war machine, the elimination of Nazi tyranny over the oppressed peoples of Europe, and security for ourselves in
the free world. – General Dwight D Eisenhower.

History records that D-Day was postponed for twenty-four hours in the hope that a break in the weather would allow the landings to take place on Tuesday 6th June 1944. On receipt of news that there would be a brief respite from the stormy conditions General Eisenhower took the brave decision to go ahead. Allied airborne units began landing just after midnight and the seaborne invasion followed up some hours later.

Planning for the invasion had started under Lieutenant-General Frederick Morgan in 1943 but it wasn't until General Sir Bernard Montgomery was appointed land forces commander for *Overlord* that he returned to the UK from Italy to take up the reins for planning the assault. Monty did not wholly approve of Morgan's COSSAC plan and beefed up the number of divisions allotted to the initial landings. He was convinced that getting the maximum number of boots on the ground would counteract what the Germans could do in response and subsequent events proved him right. The Allies' overwhelming air superiority was bound to have an impact on proceedings but the poor weather leading up to 6th June was a hindrance and it would continue to interfere with operations for some time.

Photographers from *The Times* and *Daily Sketch* were literally all at sea during the landings. Eric Greenwood was embedded aboard HMS *Scylla*, the flagship of Admiral Sir Philip Vian,

commander of the Eastern Task Force landing Anglo-Canadian forces on Sword, Juno and Gold. *Scylla* sailed sedately up and down the beaches a mile or so off shore. A frustrated Greenwood would content himself with using his regular plate camera in addition to what was termed a 'special light camera' using 120 roll film and a telephoto lens. He photographed the distant scene on shore, the naval bombardment and some unique images of events aboard *Scylla* but had to wait until the next day to get on dry land to record how the assault was fairing.

Meanwhile R. H. Clough and Frederick Skinner were also enjoying life on the ocean wave. They were attached to Royal Navy and Merchant Navy Pools recording Operation *Neptune*, the maritime element of the invasion. As with other British newspaper photographers they had no hope of getting ashore on the big day and all the best known images taken within the Anglo-Canadian landing area were made by military photographers, many of whom had come from a press background. The best known is probably Sergeant Jimmy Mapham whose work on Sword Beach has appeared on everything from books to tea towels and postage stamps.

Once on land Eric Greenwood would spend just six days witnessing the huge build-up of British and Canadian forces before heading home to England. For Clough and Skinner there would be plenty to photograph, including the

Mulberry Harbour at Arromanches, the endless procession of reinforcements and stores and the transit of German prisoners to England. Visiting entertainers would add a bit of colour and these images of the backstory to *Overlord* are immensely valuable to forming a full understanding of just how huge an undertaking the invasion was.

Before the invasion of France, Montgomery's staff had been encouraged to project phase lines for the Allied advance in Normandy predicting the area of territory that would be liberated by set dates. Monty himself had little or no interest in the necessity and left it to a staff officer to carry out but the impact of these quite arbitrary choices would discolour the campaign in Normandy. The British 3rd Infantry Division's narrow failure to reach Caen on D-Day and the subsequent month-long battle for control of the ruined city would lead to the received preception, especially in the United States, that the British were cautious and unwilling to take risks in battle.

The fact remains that heavy Anglo-Canadian infantry casualties in Normandy had a dire impact on future operations. *The Times* accurately described the fighting as a war of attrition on June 16th and there was still a long way to go. In percentage terms losses would be equal to the Somme in 1916. Veteran units from Eighth Army came to Normandy amid high expectations but were in for a rude shock, especially when they came up against the SS. The conflict in the desert against Rommel has been tagged as a 'war without hate' but in Normandy highly motivated Waffen SS and other German units would exact a heavy price from the British for any ground gained and for the Canadians there would be grisly encounters to contend with.

Some Allied planners expected the Germans to retire to the Seine to fight a battle on ground of their own choosing. Instead they fought for practically every inch of soil. Montgomery would be mired in conflict over strategy with his fellow senior commanders for the rest of the war. Although his difficult personality made him few friends amongst senior officers, he was admired by much of the British rank and file and even more so by the public at home. While his strategy for the Normandy campaign proved to be flexible and proactive his rigid adherence to the mantra that it had all gone to plan carried on well into the post-war period of the 'battle of the memoirs' undermining his success.

Recording the war for British newspapers offered diverse opportunities. Cathal O'Gorman sailed from Portsmouth aboard the cruiser HMS *Enterprise* to record the naval bombardment of Cherbourg on 25th June in support of the American ground assault on the port. German shore batteries did not go down quietly and O'Gorman had a lively time of it. A month after Eric Greenwood's adventures, Bill Warhurst arrived in time to witness the fall of Caen. Atlantic storms had delayed his arrival, but once on the ground he quickly set to work and stayed with Montgomery's 21st Army Group until the very end.

The closure of the Falaise Pocket by the Canadians and Poles on 21st August trapped the remnants of two German armies on the wrong side of the Seine. Paris was liberated by 25th August and this signalled the end of *Overlord*. A new phase of the campaign when immense distances were covered in just a few short weeks was about to begin, but there were trials to come.

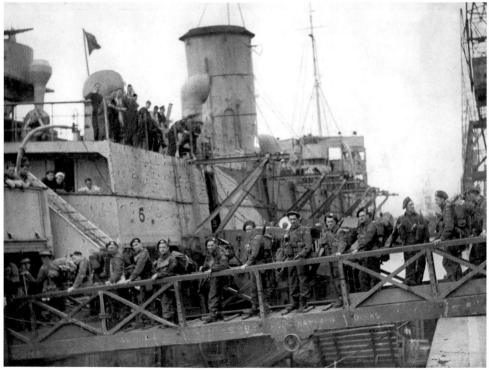

TOP Ground crew painting invasion stripes on a Mosquito VI of No 464 Squadron RAAF at RAF Gravesend. The man in the foreground is clearly making up the numbers.

Kemsley M4244R

BOTTOM Canadian assault troops of Le Regiment De la Chaudiere boarding the *Lady of Mann* at Southampton. The 'Chauds' were due to land on Nan Red at Bernieres on Juno Beach around 0830hrs but had a difficult time, losing four landing craft to mines leaving the occupants little option but to swim ashore and regroup.

Frederick R. Skinner, Kemsley print

TOP The invasion fleet sails to Normandy. Eric Greenwood of *The Times* was aboard HMS *Scylla*, the command ship of the Eastern Task Force flying the flag of Admiral Philip Vian. Trying to make something of the view on the way out did not yield anything to write home about but Greenwood's work below decks left us with some important images of the D-Day story. Officers busy charting the progress of the invasion convoys in the operational plotting room.

Eric Greenwood, The Times DD11

LEFT Later that evening the aircrew of 464 held their final briefings. Flight Lieutenant Tom McPhee DFM (right) and Flight Lieutenant Geoffrey Atkins stand over a map. Lifelong friends, McPhee and Atkins attacked various targets on D-Day and in the following weeks. They had flown together on Operation *Jericho*, the famous Amiens prison raid of February 1944.

Kemsley M4244R

TOP RIGHT This image shows the busy wireless room with coders on the left and operators on the right. The chalkboard on the right lists the various headquarters ships for assault elements of the Eastern Task Force.

Eric Greenwood, The Times DD16

BOTTOM RIGHT A less-known aspect of D-Day were the leaflet-dropping flights made by the USAAF 422nd Bombardment Squadron from Chelveston. These sorties were usually flown at night in unarmed B-17F Flying Fortresses which had their undersides painted matt black. On D-Day the squadron flew in the early dawn light and achieved their mission of dropping warning leaflets to the Normandy populace without loss. Although prepared for publication with the map obscured and under the headline 'Six who warned the French' this image taken on 8th June was 'killed' by the censor. L–R: Captain E. J. Clever, Lieutenant G. W. England, Captain A. E. Weil, Major E. J. Aber Jnr, Lieutenant W. J. Studt and Captain W. C. Melton. Earle Joseph Aber Jnr of Racine, Wisconsin was a specialist in leaflet dropping and was promoted to lieutenant colonel later in 1944. The radio broadcast of his D-Day experiences can be heard on *USAAF at War 1942–45 (vol 1)*. Sadly, he was shot down by British friendly fire and killed in March 1945. A team of divers recovered his body from the River Stour in 2000 and he is buried at Arlington National Cemetery.

Robert Chandler, Kemsley M241V

TOP LEFT The S-class destroyer HMNoS *Stord* was a veteran of the battle of the North Cape in December 1943, ending in the destruction of the German battleship *Scharnhorst*. *Stord* was one of two Norwegian destroyers in the Eastern Task Force on D-Day. The other, the *Svenner*, was sunk by German torpedo boats.

Eric Greenwood, The Times DD26

BOTTOM LEFT HMS *Warspite* lets rip, 1130hrs. Known as 'The Old Lady', she opened the bombardment of Sword Beach from 26,000 yards (23.7km) at 0500hrs on D-Day. A much-travelled and battered veteran of the battle of Jutland, she could not use all her main armament having been severely damaged by an air-launched Fritz-X wire guided glider bomb during the Italian campaign. On D-Day *Warspite* was narrowly missed by torpedoes launched by vessels from the German 5th Torpedo Flotilla, one of which sank the *Svenner*. *Warspite* continued firing on targets all day and into the next.

Eric Greenwood, The Times DD70

RIGHT 1130hrs. The modern Crown Colony-class light cruiser HMS *Mauritius* led Bombardment Force D working off Sword Beach. With her is the 1917 vintage Danae-class cruiser ORP *Dragon* transferred to the Polish Navy from the British in 1943. *Dragon* had a busy day firing on German positions and in return was hit sustaining a small number of wounded. The old ship suffered technical problems and after a stint back in Britain she returned to Normandy in July where she was hit and severely damaged by a *Neger* manned torpedo on the 8th, with the loss of 27 men. It was decided to abandon her and she was stripped of anything useful and scuttled as a breakwater for the Mulberry harbour at Arromanches on 20th July.

Eric Greenwood, The Times DD71

TOP LEFT The scene off Gold Beach aboard the Hunt-class destroyer HMS *Cottesmore*. Gunnery officer W. Evans of London (centre); signals officer I. A. Rodger of Reading (l) and Surgeon-Lieutenant W. J. Thompson of Canada (r) keep an eye on events along with two other sailors. *Cottesmore* was an escort for Assault Convoy G2. The convoy was made up of the 18th Fleet Minesweeping Flotilla and part of 150th BYMS Minesweeping Flotilla.

R. H. Clough, Kemsley M4261J

BOTTOM LEFT This view of one of the sectors of Juno Beach at around 1930hrs illustrates the challenge facing Eric Greenwood to get any usable images of the invasion from his position on HMS *Scylla*.

Eric Greenwood, The Times DD91

TOP RIGHT By the afternoon news of the invasion was the number one topic in London and beyond. Soldiers read the *Evening News* in Trafalgar Square.

Kemsley M4141G

MIDDLE RIGHT A rare survivor from the copy negatives made of artwork reporting on D-Day from the *Daily Sketch*.

Kemsley M4329S

BOTTOM RIGHT A couple pray for divine intervention at Westminster Cathedral.

Robert Chandler, Kemsley M4241Q

TOP By the late afternoon of D-Day, with thousands of men on the ground in Normandy the foundations of Allied victory in Europe began to be laid. A Phoenix caisson for one of the Mulberry harbours on its way to France.

BOTTOM Part of the plan for the naval element of the invasion, Operation *Neptune*, involved scuttling a number of elderly 'block ships' to create breakwaters off the invasion beaches. Still more were used for the two Mulberry harbours, A and B, constructed off Omaha and at Arromanches. This image shows some of the block ship crewmen arriving back in England.

R. H. Clough, Kemsley M4245R

TOP With a temporary improvement in the weather on 7th June, Eric Greenwood managed to make a short run ashore using both his light and plate cameras to record what he saw of the British build-up. Here we see a Landing Craft Tank on its run in packed with troops bound for Gold Beach.

Eric Greenwood, The Times DD131

BOTTOM A classic image of the build-up at Jig sector of Gold Beach as a convoy of DUKW amphibious trucks passes along the beach at Asnelles.

Eric Greenwood, The Times DD140

TOP A smiling Eric Greenwood at Asnelles.

The Times DD143

BOTTOM We have seen that dropping propaganda leaflets was a key part of the Allied strategy to win hearts and minds. The *Flying Dutchman* carried General Eisenhower's message for people in occupied Europe. This leaflet from 13th June has the headline 'AFTER SEVEN DAYS' and includes a large image taken on 7th June at Asnelles by Eric Greenwood.

Author

TOP 9th June 1944. A final glimpse of life aboard HMS *Scylla:* the daily officers' meeting. From second left – Rear Admiral Arthur Talbot commanding Force S; Admiral Philip Vian commanding the Eastern Task Force; behind him is Rear Admiral Frederick Dalrymple-Hamilton commanding 10th Cruiser Squadron; Commodore Geoffrey Oliver commanding Force J; Captain Thomas Brownrigg captain of the *Scylla* and Flag Captain of the Eastern Task Force. On the right looking away is Rear Admiral Wilfrid Patterson who commanded Bombardment Force D from HMS *Mauritius*. HMS *Scylla*'s role in the invasion ended on 23rd June when she was badly damaged by a mine. She was written off and scrapped in 1950.

Eric Greenwood, The Times DD194

BOTTOM On board the newly arrived HMS *Faulknor* where Admiral Vian came to meet the Allied ground forces commander General Bernard Law Montgomery and Second Army commander Lieutenant-General Miles Dempsey, 7th June 1944. Monty had been anxious to get to France and he would stay for six months before taking a short break from the campaign.

Eric Greenwood, The Times DD290

TOP Winston Churchill came out to see things for himself on 12th June. He is pictured saluting admirers in Courseulles while the Chief of the Imperial General Staff, Field Marshal Sir Alan Brooke, and the imperial heavyweight Field Marshal Jan Christian Smuts find other things to look at.

Eric Greenwood, The Times DD336

BOTTOM Even a small harbour like the one at Courseulles was useful for bringing in supplies and it was subject to air attacks by the Luftwaffe who even used *Mistel* drones, but with little impact. The task of keeping the place in working order fell to men like these from the Pioneer Corps.

Eric Greenwood, The Times DD202

TOP While Churchill was in Normandy, British casualties were pictured landing at Pitch House Jetty, Portsmouth. Gasping for a cigarette regardless of their injuries a heavily bandaged Lieutenant Reeve of Bedford and Corporal Rodgers of Burnley stop to light up.

Kemsley M4248Z

BOTTOM Churchill and his retinue mobbed by an enthusiastic crowd in Courseulles. Brooke, Monty and Vian are visible in the throng. After this Eric Greenwood returned to London and it was anticipated his replacement, Bill Warhurst, would arrive soon after, but Atlantic storms seriously disrupted the Normandy timetable and he did not arrive until 4th July.

Eric Greenwood, The Times DD332

German prisoners raise a smile for the camera in Gosport after their arrival from Normandy. Streets full of men and vehicles heading to France and the steady numbers of prisoners coming the other way were a big attraction for onlookers of all ages.

R. H. Clough, Kemsley M4245R

The light cruiser HMS *Glasgow* replenished stores and ammunition ahead of her deployment with Combined Task Force 129 for the bombardment of Cherbourg in support of US ground forces investing the port. The task force was commanded by Rear Admiral Morton Deyo, USN, and included the battleships *Arkansas*, *Nevada* and *Texas* in addition to a number of cruisers, destroyers and minesweepers. The US Army VII Corps had cut off the Cotentin Peninsula but were unable to break down defences to get into Cherbourg and naval fire support to suppress German gun emplacements was seen as an option to speed things along. Cathal O'Gorman of *The Times* sailed aboard the British light cruiser HMS *Enterprise* and filmed events on 25th June when Deyo led Group 1 of the task force, including *Glasgow*, into battle. These images show *Glasgow* at Portsmouth on the 12th where her cheerful crew were ready for action as cordite containers came aboard

Kemsley M4244R

The battle of Cherbourg. A sequence of three images showing HMS *Glasgow* straddled and then hit on her hangar deck by German fire just after 1220hrs. Although she suffered no deaths several men were injured but the most serious issue was the severe damage to *Glasgow* herself. As a result of the action at Cherbourg she took no further part in the European war but was repaired in time to head out to the Pacific a year later.

Cathal O'Gorman, The Times CG389, CG387, CG388

TOP O'Gorman photographed several other warships and this image of the Gleaves-class destroyer USS *Emmons* speeding past HMS *Enterprise* is representative. After Normandy she made her way to the Pacific where she formed part of the anti-aircraft picket defending the naval task force landing marines on Okinawa on 6th April 1945. The picket were heavily engaged by kamikaze aircraft and in going to the aid of the battered USS *Rodman* the *Emmons* was struck by five aircraft in a simultaneous attack with the loss of sixty dead and over seventy wounded. Completely wrecked but still afloat, she was sunk the next day.

Cathal O'Gorman, The Times CG394

BOTTOM A pre-war portrait of *The Times* photographer Cathal O'Gorman who took the photos of the battle of Cherbourg. On 23rd July he was with his wife Agnes and stepson John at the home of Agnes' sister Stella in Wandsworth when a V1 flying bomb hit the property. Agnes, John and Stella were killed along with several neighbours. Cathal O'Gorman remained on *The Times* staff until his retirement but he was greatly affected by the incident and is said to have occasionally wandered off from events he was covering or would just disappear now and again. The paper stood by him and he continued to produce work of the highest standard for the remainder of his career.

The Times 34615

LEFT *Babbler*, a Churchill MkVI from 'B' Squadron, 107th Regiment Royal Armoured Corps, leading a column of tanks of 34th Armoured Brigade pictured on the brigade's first full day in Normandy on 4th July 1944. The 34th had been delayed by the stormy weather that disrupted the Allied build-up, destroying or damaging the two Mulberry harbours built after D-Day. The terrible weather had also delayed the arrival of Bill Warhurst and this image is from the first sequence he took after getting ashore. Bill had always enjoyed an affinity with rural scenes; so adding tanks just gave him something else to do well.

Herbert W. Warhurst, The Times WN5017

RIGHT Infantrymen of the 6th Battalion North Staffordshire Regiment pass dead Germans on a road outside La Bijude on the outskirts of Caen, 9th July 1944. The battalion were part of 176th Infantry Brigade of 59th Infantry Division and took part in Operation *Charnwood*, the latest attempt by Montgomery to capture the city, supported by heavy bombing. The attack went in on 8th July with the assaulting infantry suffering badly in a fight that lasted into the next day. This image was taken at a time when clearing pockets of resistance was still going on and it illustrates Bill Warhurst's determination to see action. Caen had fallen at last.

Herbert W. Warhurst, The Times WN5038

TOP Shermans of 27th Armoured Brigade move out of a ruined orchard at La Bijude during the closing stages of Operation *Charnwood*, on 9th July 1944.

Herbert W. Warhurst, The Times WN5047

BOTTOM LEFT Men from C Company, 2nd Battalion Royal Ulster Rifles look at a road sign to Paris amid the devastation of Caen. To the left is Sergeant Robert John Rainey who was awarded the Military Medal in 1945. On the right is Lieutenant Cyril Rand. He was wounded at Troarn later in July and rose to the rank of major while serving with the London Irish Rifles after the war.

Herbert W. Warhurst, The Times WN5068

BOTTOM RIGHT Caen was in ruins. *Herbert W. Warhurst, The Times WN5066*

TOP One person attracted to the destruction of Caen was the Official War Artist Lieutenant Thomas Hennell, RNVR. He was denied the opportunity to go ashore on D-Day and so he sought every opportunity to illustrate the war up close. At the end of the European war Hennell made his way out to the Far East where he remained after the Japanese surrender. He was in Java during the period of growing violence by Indonesian nationalists and was last seen on 5th November 1945 being dragged away by a mob. His body was never found. An artist held in high regard, his name is recorded on the Chatham Naval Memorial.

Herbert W. Warhurst, The Times WN5069

BOTTOM LEFT The communities ringing Caen suffered considerable damage during the battle for the city. Here the local Resistance leader brings food supplies to the inhabitants of what is left of Fleury-sur-Orne, a village that had been renamed during the Great War in honour of its namesake obliterated during the battle of Verdun in 1916.

Herbert W. Warhurst, The Times WN5156

BOTTOM RIGHT Refugees from the fighting at Caen living in a quarry near Fleury-sur-Orne.

Herbert W. Warhurst, The Times WN5201

TOP LEFT Tank losses in Normandy often exceeded expectations and the recovery and repair of damaged armour was a never-ending process for the men of the Royal Electrical and Mechanical Engineers. Bill Warhurst spent time recording men at a REME workshop where refurbishment work was under way. This image shows a Sherman tank on the back of a Scammell Pioneer transporter delivered to the workshop at Basly. Note the difference between the cast and welded-hull variants of Shermans.

Herbert W. Warhurst, The Times WN5173

BOTTOM LEFT REME mechanics repair a tank engine. The Continental R-957 radial engine powered both the M4 and M4A1 Sherman. The power plant was adapted from an aero-engine developed by Wright. Continental built over 53,000 of these engines for use in armoured vehicles.

Herbert W. Warhurst, The Times WN5175

RIGHT Track repairs were physically demanding work.

Herbert W. Warhurst, The Times WN5176

LEFT The supply of new tanks from the UK continued throughout the Normandy campaign. Three factory-fresh Sherman Hybrid Firefly Ic tanks reverse on to a tank landing ship on the hardway at Gosport. The tank was armed with a QF 17-pounder gun capable of taking on the German Panther and Tiger I and it proved to be an essential addition to British armoured regiments. The Firefly Ic was made by fitting together sections of cast- and welded-hull models of the M4 Sherman with the co-driver position removed to create the room for a gun and ammunition that were much bigger than standard armament.

R. H. Clough, Kemsley M4245Q

TOP RIGHT The undoubted engineering marvel of *Overlord* were the two prefabricated Mulberry harbours, A at Omaha and B at Arromanches, over which tens of thousands of tons of stores and equipment arrived in theatre. Atrocious weather would have a dire impact on Allied preparations when the harbour at Omaha was destroyed in the 'great storm' that began on 19th June lasting for three days. The harbour at Arromanches, which acquired the name Port Winston, survived and remained in use for months to come. Its remains are a tourist attraction to this day.

R. H. Clough, Kemsley M4248H

BOTTOM RIGHT This view shows the network of piers on Mulberry B at Arromanches. The *Samark* was built in 1943 as the *John G. North* but transferred to Britain under Lend-Lease and renamed. Ellerman's Wilson Line of Hull operated her on behalf of the Ministry of War Transport. *Samark* was returned to the USA after the war and reverted to her original name. She was scrapped in 1960.

R. H. Clough, Kemsley M4248H

LEFT Crewmen from the elderly coaster *Oranmore* relax after another trip to Normandy carrying fuel supplies on 11th August 1944. The coaster, which dated back to 1895, was a coal carrier converted to haul petrol. She was severely damaged by a mine 10 miles off Normandy on one trip but continued on her journey and made subsequent trips after repair. Her master Herbert Henson of Sunderland was awarded an MBE for his leadership.

Frederick R. Skinner, Kemsley M4245Q

TOP RIGHT This un-named Liberty ship was one of many vessels that fell victim to mines during the Normandy campaign. *Frederick R. Skinner, Kemsley M4244R*

BOTTOM RIGHT Ships of all shapes and sizes were involved in the supply effort including the rescue tug HMS *Sabine*. She is pictured meeting up with the Assurance-class tug HMS *Griper*. *Sabine* had appeared in the popular pre-war movie *Tugboat Annie* featuring Wallace Beery and Marie Dressler before finding her way to Britain where she was refitted and taken up for naval service by the Admiralty at the start of the war. *Sabine* had started life as the *Freeport Sulphur II* in 1917 and was scrapped on the Tyne in 1950. *Kemsley M4244Q*

LEFT The British were plagued by manpower shortages as a result of the attritional fighting in Normandy. These men of the 24th Lancers enjoying a musical interlude on 23rd July would see their regiment disbanded within days to provide reinforcements for others.

Herbert Warhurst, The Times WN5211

TOP RIGHT Landmines were an omnipresent hazard for the Allies in Normandy. Here men of the 15th (Scottish) Division take care in a sunken road near Sept-Vents.

Herbert W. Warhurst, The Times WN5244

BOTTOM RIGHT A number of film and variety stars provided entertainment for the armed forces through ENSA – the Entertainment National Service Association. Here George Formby and wife Beryl perform for the crew of HMS *Ambitious* on 23rd July.

Kemsley M4244Q

LEFT There are few smiles on the faces of these men of the Monmouthshire Regiment on the last day of July.

Herbert W. Warhurst, The Times WN5259

TOP RIGHT A 6-pounder anti-tank gun of 15th (Scottish) Division guarding the road at St Martin-des-Besaces.

Herbert W. Warhurst, The Times WN5290

BOTTOM RIGHT Shermans of the Guards Armoured Division roll on towards Le Beny-Bocage.

Herbert W. Warhurst, The Times WN5301

TOP *The Times* correspondent Bob Cooper and other journalists are greeted by recently liberated villagers at Le Beny-Bocage.

Herbert W. Warhurst, The Times WN6234

BOTTOM Given German reliance on equine transport it was inevitable that horses would be bear the brunt of the Allied onslaught. Anti-tank gunners with their Loyd Carriers are pictured at a scene typical of the German retreat from Normandy at St Charles-de-Percy.

Herbert W. Warhurst, The Times WN5316

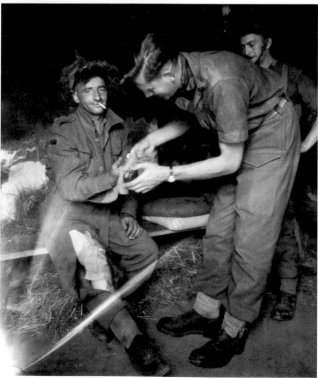

Casualties of the 59th (Staffordshire) Division are treated at an aid post set up in a farmhouse near Grimbosq. With its coalmining region connections the 59th was often referred to as the 'Pithead' Division.

Herbert W. Warhurst, The Times WN5370 and WN5377

TOP A 'join up' image of the advance along the Caen–Falaise road showing the village of Rocquancourt under fire on the right.

Herbert W. Warhurst, The Times WN5383A

BOTTOM Two abandoned StuG III assault guns of Sturmgeschutz Abteilung 1344 at Tilly-la-Campagne. The village was captured by 51st (Highland) Division on 8th August.

Herbert W. Warhurst, The Times WN5402

BOTTOM The Germans abandoned a headquarters in a quarry near Tilly leaving several vehicles that were quickly snapped up by these men of the 1st Battalion Queen's Own Cameron Highlanders of Canada.

Herbert W. Warhurst, The Times WN5404

LEFT BL 4.2inch mortar men of the 7th Battalion Royal Northumberland Fusiliers firing on enemy positions during a German counter-attack on Thury-Harcourt, 12th August 1944. It was the scene of such intense fighting that heavy losses suffered by battalions of the 59th (Staffordshire) Division led to its disbandment on 21st August.

Herbert W. Warhurst, The Times WN5433

TOP RIGHT Men of 2nd Battalion Gloucestershire Regiment take cover outside Thury-Harcourt on 14th August during a period of counter-attacks by the Germans. The battalion served in 56th Infantry Brigade, part of the 49th (West Riding) Division.

Herbert W. Warhurst, The Times WN5440A

BOTTOM RIGHT The 59th (Staffordshire) Division had advanced near Le Haut d'Ouilly on 15th August where Major-General Lewis Lyne is pictured holding an orders group with the brigadiers of the division. Following the disbandment of his division Lyne was given command of the 50th (Northumbrian) Division, but this, too, was disbanded to provide men for other depleted units in December 1944. Major-General Lyne moved on to command 7th Armoured Division, leading it to garrison Berlin just after the war.

Herbert W. Warhurst, The Times WN5470

TOP AND TOP MIDDLE Bill Warhurst visited a psychological warfare unit and photographed men preparing leafleting shells to fire on German positions. These shells are for a 25-pounder gun. He also photographed a unit using an Austin K2 fitted with loudspeakers to call on the enemy to surrender. Warhurst advised that this sequence of negatives would have to be censored by the Ministry of Information and this proved to be the case because the MoI withheld a number of plates that were never returned.

Herbert W. Warhurst, The Times WN5480 and WN5482

TOP RIGHT The horror of what the Germans called the *Rückmarsch* could be seen on just about any road where retreating vehicles were caught by Allied aircraft or ground units. The unfortunate crew of a Hummel self-propelled gun bear testament to the disaster experienced by the Germans in Normandy.

Herbert W. Warhurst, The Times WN5541

BOTTOM MIDDLE After their disastrous counter-offensive at Mortain that began on 7th August, the Germans were in full retreat and the race to trap the remnants of Seventh Army and Fifth Panzer Army in the Falaise Pocket was on. Although thousands of men and some vehicles escaped across the River Seine, the best part of 300,000 Germans were casualties or made prisoner in Normandy. Hundreds of vehicles were destroyed by Allied bombers or just abandoned by the retreating Germans in their rush to escape. In this image, wary Canadian troops pass by a burned-out Tiger I on the Trun–Argentan road. Mines and booby-traps remained a constant threat.

Herbert W. Warhurst, The Times WN5493

BOTTOM RIGHT The battle of the Falaise Pocket lasted from 12th–21st August and although as many as 50,000 Germans escaped, the closure of the pocket by Polish and Canadian units signalled complete defeat for Hitler's armies in Normandy. Bill Warhurst was in Trun on 18th August where he took this image of the post office burning while Canadian troops rounded up stragglers.

Herbert W. Warhurst, The Times WN5504

TOP LEFT A busy scene in Chambois on 23rd August where vehicles of the 50th (Northumbrian) Division pass infantry of the 43rd (Wessex) Division while American troops travel the other way using captured German trucks. The '41' tactical sign on the Universal Carrier and the half-track following behind denote the 61st Reconnaissance Regiment.

Herbert W. Warhurst, The Times WN5536

BOTTOM LEFT An extraordinary sight for the British passing through Chambois was this group of mounted American troops who were content to ham it up for Bill Warhurst showing off captured pistols while riding German horses. The use of ad hoc mounted troops was found to be a useful expedient by some American units in Normandy. The vehicles are from the 4th Battalion Wiltshire Regiment and 110th (Dorset) Light Anti-Aircraft Regiment, Royal Artillery.

Herbert W. Warhurst, The Times WN5541B

TOP RIGHT To the victors the spoils: men from an unidentified unit rifling through abandoned German vehicles and equipment outside Chambois.

Herbert W. Warhurst, The Times WN5541F

BOTTOM RIGHT *Daily Sketch* war correspondent Bill Makin died of wounds sustained in an ambush on 15th August when he and his colleague Alexander McGowan of the *New York Sun* encountered German tanks while travelling in a jeep. The Germans took the two reporters prisoner and transported Makin some distance for treatment for a stomach wound but he died on 26th August and is buried at Villeneuve-St Georges. The Great War veteran Makin was 48 years old.

Albert Abrahams, Kemsley M4240S

An abandoned Panther tank from SS-Panzer Regiment 12 forms the background as young and old celebrate the arrival of troops in Elbeuf on the River Seine on 27th August. Further upriver the fall of Paris signalled the end of Operation *Overlord*. The Normandy campaign was over and the race across France into Belgium was about to begin.

Herbert W. Warhurst, The Times WN5585

MIXED FORTUNES

———————

The Allied breakout from Normandy triggered advances of breathtaking speed across France with the Americans in Omar Bradley's recently activated 12th Army Group rushing towards the German frontier while Montgomery's 21st Army Group swept on towards Brussels and Antwerp.

Montgomery increasingly favoured concentrating the Allied armies to form a single thrust into Germany but Eisenhower demurred, favouring a broad front approach whereby the full length of the German defences would be under constant pressure. To support this, a second invasion took place on 15th August, this time in the South of France. There were bitter arguments between the British and Americans over this strategy and the original codename for the landings, *Anvil*, was changed to *Dragoon*, allegedly at the behest of Churchill to show he had been forced into accepting it. Whatever Monty and the British high command thought at the time, *Dragoon* offered the potential to deploy a second American-led army group to roll up the Germans. With the possession of more ports American divisions could be deployed directly from the United States. By the end of the war there would be five US field armies operating in North-West Europe.

Port facilities were vital to the Allied cause and with this in mind the Canadian First Army were tasked with capturing Le Havre and Dieppe before moving on to the Channel ports. For the Canadians the prospect of a return to Dieppe held strong emotions given bitter memories of the disastrous raid of August 1942. The town was captured on 1st September. Rouen had fallen a day earlier and on this occasion Bill Warhurst enjoyed the glory of entering the city in advance of the leading troops. The port of Le Havre was devastated by Allied bombing, causing the deaths of thousands of civilians and the destruction of over 12,000 buildings. Regardless of this the Germans held on but the city fell to I British Corps on 12th September.

The Channel ports would prove to be a tough obstacle but the Canadians pressed on although their commander Lieutenant-General Harry Crerar came in for criticism over the 'slow' handling of his forces from Montgomery and others. The fact Crerar was suffering from dysentery may have been a mitigating factor but he was anxious to limit what he saw as needless casualties. Boulogne had been declared to be a fortress by Adolf Hitler, but the Canadians took the heavily bombed port on 22nd September. Calais came in for similar treatment and the capture of the port combined with the reduction of numerous coastal batteries by 1st October brought to an end the near constant bombardment of Dover that had lasted four years.

The German coastal batteries mounted guns taken from French warships and they used railway guns that could be shuttled around to hide from Allied aircraft. One enthusiastic German news report from June 1944 claimed the guns had bombarded Maidstone, damaging invasion shipping. A rebuttal in *The Times* pointed out the town was 57 miles from the guns and consequently some way out of range, however shell fragments from a 210mm railway gun *were* found near Chatham, 55 miles from the French coast. The massive Lindemann battery near Sangatte was buried under Channel Tunnel spoil in the 1980s but other casemates around Calais remain open for careful inspection, a testament to the vast but ultimately futile construction effort made by the Germans to build their Atlantic Wall. *The Times* reported on the last occasions German batteries fired on Dover and the *Daily Sketch* was there to see the relief and celebrations in the town when the guns were finally silenced.

Dunkerque proved to be altogether more difficult to take. The Canadians failed to break down the German defences and the decision was taken to mask the town while the advance continued leaving the port covered by the 1st Czechoslovak Armoured Brigade. The belligerent Germans held out until the end of the war and they did not surrender to the Czechs until 9th May 1945.

As the Canadians advanced into Belgium the British Second Army raced across the battlefields of the Great War along roads used by two British Expeditionary Forces that enjoyed different fortunes in 1918 and 1940. The army advanced on an axis of Amiens and Arras aiming for Antwerp. Ever mindful that lines of communications were overly extended, the port was seen as a crucial objective by Eisenhower. Arras fell to the Guards Armoured Division on 3rd September and one officer was happy to recover kit he had had to abandon in 1940. The following day Brussels was liberated, amid tumultuous scenes.

The British advanced to the Dutch-Belgian border amid a premature euphoria within the Allied command that the war might be over before the year was out. But already signs of a loss of momentum were evident. The British had covered 250 miles in just a few weeks and Montgomery's armies needed to rest. The advance guard were at the end of a supply line extending perilously all the way back to Normandy. Although the vast port of Antwerp was captured intact on the 4th, Monty allowed his tired army to halt. The vital approaches to the port along the Scheldt were not cleared of German resistance and this is rightly seen as one of the great mistakes of the campaign. A large part of General Gustav-Adolf von Zangen's Fifteenth Army was allowed to escape and would have to be dealt with later. It was an error that would cost the Allies dear in the months to come.

Logistical problems and the exhaustion of the troops contributed to a reverse in fortunes as the advance ran out of steam. On top of this German resistance was beginning to stiffen as the Nazis recovered from their disaster in Normandy. Eisenhower had assumed direct command of the Allied field armies on 1st September, a move dismissed by a contemptuous Montgomery who thought little of his abilities as a tactician. That same day the British press reported Monty's promotion to field marshal. Monty's habit of seeing things in purely military terms and his failure to appreciate the importance of American public opinion set him at odds with Eisenhower's strategy. The diminishing role of Britain within the alliance created tensions as Montgomery, encouraged by his boss at home Field Marshal Sir Alan Brooke, sought to maintain, if not enhance, his position and the standing of his armies within the alliance.

Instead of dealing with the Scheldt Monty fixed his gaze on the Ruhr and amid the disagreements with Eisenhower over priorities he got his wish, opening the door for Operation *Market Garden*. The audacity of Monty's plan to seize bridges over the Maas, Waal and Neder Rijn as part of a rapid advance to the Ruhr has been described as out of character but the bold concept met with serious difficulties at the planning stage when senior airmen dictated the location of the drop zones for the British airborne assault on Arnhem. They were a worrying distance from the crucial bridge, leaving Roy Urquhart's 1st British Airborne Division a great deal to do.

Even worse, in their haste to get into the fight British planners dismissed the presence of the understrength but veteran II SS Panzer Corps. The oversight would contribute to the disaster facing the British Airborne. A succession of cancelled operations had left the restless 1st British Airborne Division in particular itching to get at the Germans before it was too late. *Market Garden* would confer lasting glory on the three airborne divisions involved, but for the British it would end in heartbreak.

The ground plan, the advance of the veteran XXX Corps along a single highway linking Eindhoven, Nijmegen and Arnhem was itself fraught with potential difficulties and the projection that it would take Major General Sir Brian Horrocks' units 48 hours to travel the sixty-odd miles to Arnhem proved wide of the mark.

Bill Tetlow photographed preparations for the aerial assault and flew to the Netherlands in a Short Stirling tug on that fateful Sunday 17th September. He could consider himself lucky to have got back in one piece. Meanwhile Bill Warhurst was with XXX Corps heading for Eindhoven. He witnessed the first of many blocking actions by the Germans and he put himself at some risk throughout the operation. As the advance progressed he arrived in Eindhoven to photograph the joyous scenes as the British column struggled through the city and moved on towards Nijmegen. By this time the fate of the 1st British Airborne Division hung in the balance as the offensive power of two SS panzer divisions and the rapid reaction of other units began to exact a terrible price for the planners' errors of judgement.

Warhurst was in Nijmegen just after the epic capture of the bridges there by the US 82nd Airborne and Guards Armoured Division but by this time the fate of the men holding their end of the bridge at Arnhem was sealed. The last of John Frost's force at the bridge were being mopped up. Only the Germans heard their final radio message, 'Out of ammunition, God Save the King.' Meanwhile the remnants of Urquhart's battered division withdrew into a defensive perimeter at Oosterbeek. Bill Tetlow returned to the Netherlands when he flew into the makeshift landing ground at Keent with American C-47 crews on the 26th. The mission to deliver medical and logistical supplies to the remnants of the 1st Airborne was an illustration of Allied air power. But *Market Garden* was dead and its failure contributed to the suffering of the people left in Nazi-occupied Holland as the Germans tightened their grip. Robert Chandler of the *Daily Sketch* pictured Roy Urquhart's sad return to Britain where the exhausted general put on a brave face.

Monty's contention that the operation was 'ninety per cent successful' ignored the reality that the failure to take the bridge at Arnhem doomed the entire enterprise. Instead it underlined the reality that a rapid advance into Germany by 21st Army Group was out of the question. The coming winter would see Monty's armies having to bludgeon their way across the Netherlands and into the Reich, fighting in terrible conditions.

LEFT With the port of Cherbourg now open the logistical headache facing Eisenhower's armies eased a little but access to other ports was vital and Antwerp remained the great prize. This typical scene shows a Liberty ship having supplies unloaded into GMC AFKWX-353 trucks.

Eric Greenwood, The Times DD421

TOP RIGHT The preponderance of Americans within the alliance had become reality in July and many more were set to arrive. As in all armies, combat troops were always the 'tip of the spear' but thousands more were needed to perform essential tasks. A large number of African Americans had been encouraged into uniform by the likes of the boxer Joe Louis who had said 'Lots of things wrong with America, but Hitler won't fix 'em.' Although the vast majority of them were employed in supporting roles rather than the combat arms, there were many well-documented exceptions. Organisations such as the famous 'Red Ball Express' delivering supplies to the front line could not have operated without the African American soldiers who drove the trucks and did so much of the manual work. Segregation was a fact of US Army life as the arrival of these nurses in Glasgow illustrates perfectly. They were clearly a source of scrutiny, official and otherwise. The meagre original caption reports they were the first African American nurses to deploy from the USA.

Kemsley M4246A

BOTTOM RIGHT The Allies had destroyed the French railway system in a bid to interdict the movement of German forces. Now it was necessary to get the network up and running as much as possible. To this end a large number of locomotives and rolling stock were manufactured in the United States and delivered to France. Here a Whitcomb 65 ton diesel electric locomotive is unloaded from HMS *Twickenham,* a former railway ferry, on 17th August. A crane gantry had been installed in January 1944 for the purpose and the ship could transport sixteen engines and rolling stock. *Twickenham* was returned to her peacetime owners after the war and stayed in service until 1974.

Frederick R. Skinner, Kemsley M4244Q

TOP LEFT The race across France was underway but there was still time to reflect on the price that had been paid for the great victory in Normandy. This is the Canadian war cemetery at Bretteville-sur-Laize.

Herbert W. Warhurst, The Times WN5472

BOTTOM LEFT War trophies have been collected since time immemorial. This Canadian warrant officer of the Stormont, Dundas and Glengarry Highlanders seems pleased with the pennant from the car of Generalleutnant Erwin Menny, the commander of 84.Infanterie-Division who was captured at Trun. Two of the men shown are wearing the MkIII helmet issued in time for the Normandy landings. Versions of it stayed in British use well into the 1980s. 27th August 1944.

Herbert W. Warhurst, The Times WN5597

RIGHT Vehicles of the Canadian First Army cross the River Seine at Vernon.
Herbert W. Warhurst, The Times WN5610

Another landmark day during the campaign came on 31st August with the liberation of Rouen. This image shows men of 1st Battalion Royal Winnipeg Rifles – the *Little Black Devils* – entering the heavily damaged city.

Herbert W. Warhurst, The Times WN5623

Bill Warhurst drives into Rouen accompanied by members of the Resistance. His account of how he and the *Daily Herald* photographer Jack Esten entered the city ahead of Canadian troops appeared in *The Times House Journal* in September 1944. 'We went into Rouen before the troops went in. There were Germans about and it was all very thrilling, if foolhardy, but we had a wonderful reception – flowers, kisses and champagne.' The two photographers made their way to the Hotel de Ville where an enthusiastic crowd surrounded them.

The Times WN6233

TOP Huge amounts of destroyed and abandoned German vehicles and equipment confronted the Rouennais upon the liberation of their city. A soldier can be seen rummaging in the remains of a Schwimmwagen bottom left.

Herbert W. Warhurst, The Times WN5634

BOTTOM A British survey estimated that, in their haste to escape, the Germans had abandoned 20 armoured fighting vehicles, 48 artillery pieces and 660 other vehicles on the south bank of the Seine at Rouen. This figure formed just a fraction of the 12,000 vehicles of all types the Germans are thought to have lost south of the Seine since 6th June.

Herbert W. Warhurst, The Times WB5641

TOP The British raced north advancing on the axis of Amiens and Arras on their way to Brussels and Antwerp. They liberated Arras on 3rd September. That same day groups of collaborators, including these women, were marched through the city by their vengeful neighbours. The photographer adjusting his camera on the right is Warhurst's colleague Jack Esten of the *Daily Herald*.

Herbert W. Warhurst, The Times
WN5655

BOTTOM After Arras the British 'motored' on towards Belgium with flags flying. A column of Sexton self-propelled guns of 153rd (Leicestershire Yeomanry) Field Regiment cruise along roads typical of the Artois battlefields of the Great War.

Herbert W. Warhurst, The Times
WN5662

TOP On the next day leading elements of the Guards Armoured Division arrived in Brussels. Divisional commander Major-General Allan Adair had sanctioned a race to see who would get there first and the Welsh Guards won. Here a Cromwell tank of 'A' Squadron 2nd Armoured Recce Battalion Welsh Guards is mobbed as it drives through the suburbs of the Belgian capital.

Herbert W. Warhurst, The Times WN5675

BOTTOM The city's Burgomaster, Joseph Vandemeulebroeck, had escaped imprisonment and immediately resumed his role in charge of the capital as the Germans departed. A special moment came when he greeted Brigadier Jean-Baptiste Piron of 1st Belgian Infantry Brigade, the *Brigade Piron.*

Herbert W. Warhurst, The Times WN5682

TOP LEFT Brussels, 4th September 1944. A Grenadier Guards Cromwell tank drives into the city centre.
Herbert W. Warhurst, The Times WN5683

BOTTOM LEFT The prize – the vast port of Antwerp pictured on 5th September 1944.
Herbert W. Warhurst, The Times WN5698

RIGHT A Short Stirling V of No138 (Special Duties) Squadron RAF drops arms to the White Brigade, a large resistance organisation run by Marcel Louette who went by the codename *Fidello*. The group had assisted the British in capturing the port of Antwerp.
Herbert W. Warhurst, The Times WN5712.

LEFT Instead of concentrating on clearing the Scheldt Estuary, Montgomery fixed his gaze on the Ruhr and was given the green light to launch Operation *Market Garden*, the combined land and airborne assault to secure bridges over a series of waterways to allow a rapid advance into the heart of the German industrial region. While crossings on the Maas and Waal were critical to the operation, it is largely defined by the fate of the British 1st Airborne Division at Arnhem. The huge aerial armada carrying the leading elements of three divisions left British bases on the morning of Sunday 17th September 1944. Bill Tetlow flew out in a Short Stirling glider tug from RAF Harwell. This image shows a briefing for men of the Glider Pilot Regiment and RAF aircrew. It was not published until 27th September 1944, having been passed by the censor two days earlier. The image caption only refers to the successful capture of the Nijmegen Bridge without any reference to Arnhem.

H. William Tetlow, Kemsley M4248G

RIGHT Aircrew collecting their flight rations.

H. William Tetlow, Kemsley M4248G

TOP LEFT A *Market Garden* image rarely seen in full frame. Men of 7th Battalion King's Own Scottish Borderers await orders to board their gliders at RAF Down Ampney on 17th September. It has an image caption referring to 'Some of the British Paratroops, grim and determined before taking off in the gliders seen in the background that took them to Holland on D-Day.' There is plenty to confuse the modern-day reader there! D-Day, of course, refers to the first day of *Market Garden* with the longstanding use of the code name for the first day of a major operation. The name had not yet become as synonymous with 6th June 1944 as it is today.

H. William Tetlow, Kemsley M4248G

TOP RIGHT Lieutenant-General Frederick 'Boy' Browning flew to the Netherlands with his 1st Airborne Corps headquarters from RAF Harwell on the 17th. He has not escaped criticism for taking up 36 gliders to deliver his large headquarters to the Netherlands. Bill Tetlow travelled out aboard a Stirling IV of No 570 Squadron RAF towing a Horsa glider of Browning's HQ.

H. William Tetlow, Kemsley M4248G

BOTTOM LEFT 'Boy' Browning pictured a month after *Market Garden*. He was known for his immaculate turn out.
Robert Chandler, Kemsley M4249Z

BOTTOM RIGHT A young officer following the fortunes of *Market Garden* was Captain Derek van den Bogaerde of the Queen's Regiment. He worked in photographic interpretation at Second Army Headquarters. Bill Warhurst photographed him on a couple of occasions because he happened to be the son of his boss, *The Times* art editor. In later life Dirk Bogarde played 'Boy' Browning in Richard Attenborough's film adaptation of Cornelius Ryan's *A Bridge Too Far* telling the story of Operation *Market Garden*.
Herbert W. Warhurst, The Times WN6224

THE LIBERATION OF EUROPE 1944–1945

TOP LEFT A Stirling tug and its Airspeed Horsa glider fly above a dramatic layer of cloud on their way to the Netherlands on 17th September. This image only survives in print form.

H. William Tetlow, Kemsley M4248G

BOTTOM LEFT Another view from Tetlow's Stirling looking down on inundated countryside. Although Browning's headquarters also used the type, the Waco CG-4 glider train in the distance is more likely to be from the US 82nd Airborne Division heading for Nijmegen.

H. William Tetlow, Kemsley M4248G

RIGHT RAF Stirlings of No 570 and No 295 Squadrons at Harwell. It is unclear if this image was taken before or after their flights to the Netherlands on the 17th. None of the aircraft shown were lost on the first day of *Market Garden* although both squadrons would suffer losses over the course of the whole operation.

H. William Tetlow, Kemsley M4248G

Pursuant with Monty's vision for *Market Garden*, the armour of XXX Corps began to roll over Joe's Bridge on the Bocholt-Herentals canal at Neerpelt in the mid-afternoon. Bill Warhurst was there to witness the kick-off with his colleague Jack Esten and a couple of army photographers. If ever there was such a day, Sunday 17th September was the one when Warhurst truly found the action he craved. This may well be one of his best-known images from the North-West Europe campaign.

Herbert W. Warhurst, The Times WN5716

TOP LEFT Much less familiar is this shot of tanks on the opposite side of the Bailey bridge.
Herbert W. Warhurst, The Times WN5714

TOP RIGHT Leading tanks of the Irish Guards had not got very far when they were fired on by anti-tank weapons operated by men of Kampfgruppe Walther – a mixed Waffen SS and paratrooper unit. The Germans knocked out nine tanks within a few minutes. A short time later Bill Warhurst approached the scene and took considerable risks to get this and other images during the battle taking place. His courage that afternoon earned him a mention in the Irish Guards regimental history for his arrival caused some amusement. 'Into the midst of the confusion amid the rockets, shells, tanks and Germans, drove a large saloon car. It was *The Times* staff photographer, as imperturbable as *The Times* ought to be.' This Sherman of No1 Squadron was at the rear of two groups of knocked-out tanks.
Herbert W. Warhurst, The Times WN5721

BOTTOM RIGHT Irish Guards armour attempting to outflank the German blocking positions. The large fire on the left is a burning grain store at Odiliahoeve Farm.
Herbert W. Warhurst, The Times WN5725

The Irish Guards go in hard. The crew of a knocked-out self-propelled gun were coerced at pistol point to identify other German positions as the Irish dealt with the ambush. This version of the original image had been prepared for publication.

Herbert W. Warhurst, The Times WN5719A

LEFT Infantry move forward to mop up resistance. Bill Warhurst stood on the roof of his car to take this image while bullets and Panzerfaust rounds were still flying about. An officer suggested he get down before he was killed and he quickly saw sense.
Herbert W. Warhurst, The Times WN5724

TOP RIGHT German prisoners working as stretcher-bearers. These men are all Luftwaffe personnel. The burning Loyd Carrier in the background was destroyed when a German prisoner lobbed a hidden grenade into it.

Herbert W. Warhurst, The Times WN5722

BOTTOM RIGHT Men of the 2nd Battalion Devonshire Regiment set out to mop up the flanks behind the Irish Guards. Bill Warhurst followed them in, taking this image close to where three Cromwell tanks of the 15th/19th Hussars detonated mines as they passed over them.

Herbert W. Warhurst, The Times WN5717

TOP LEFT With their route now open the Guards moved on to Valkenswaard where the decision to halt for the night has come in for much criticism both at the time and since. Although the Irish Guards – who had done the day's fighting – deserved a rest, other units could have pressed on to Eindhoven but it was not to be and precious time was lost. This image shows the Irish Guards about to resume their advance the following morning.
Herbert W. Warhurst, The Times WN5727

BOTTOM LEFT Guardsmen admiring a policeman's leather jacket in Valkenswaard.
Herbert W. Warhurst, The Times WN5731

RIGHT The British advance, already behind schedule, was much delayed by huge crowds celebrating in Eindhoven. Although XXX Corps linked up with the US 101st Airborne Division in the city Bill Warhurst did not photograph any American paratroopers there.
Herbert W. Warhurst, The Times WN5737

TOP LEFT On the afternoon of the 20th Warhurst was on hand to photograph the resupply mission for the 82nd Airborne at Oversasselt carried out by C-47s of 53rd Wing of IX Troop Carrier Command USAAF.

Herbert W. Warhurst, The Times WN5750

TOP RIGHT The action moves on to Nijmegen where the epic crossing of the River Waal by men of the 3rd Battalion 504th Parachute Infantry Regiment of the US 82nd Airborne Division took place in the late afternoon of 20th September. Tanks of the 2nd Tank Battalion Grenadier Guards crossed the Nijmegen road bridge to link up with the Americans who had reached the northern end while the adjacent railway bridge was also secured. It was an astonishing feat of arms. No photographs of the tank action exist but Bill Warhurst took several images of armour crossing the road bridge early on the 21st. This shot shows a nice view towards the railway bridge and the section of waterway where the airborne troops crossed the river.

Herbert W. Warhurst, The Times WN5761

BOTTOM RIGHT To the incredulity of the Americans the Guards tanks halted after taking the bridge and did not push on to Arnhem as the late afternoon light faded. The sound reason given was the need to bring up infantry because the tanks, running low on fuel and ammunition, could not go unsupported into built-up areas. The Americans were convinced the risk was worth taking. More precious time to link up with the men clinging on at Arnhem was lost and Monty's daring plan faced agonising failure. Another image from the 21st this time showing Guards half-tracks crossing the road bridge still littered with German dead.

Herbert W. Warhurst, The Times WN5754

TOP LEFT A 6-pounder anti-tank gun of the Irish Guards using the concrete roadblock on the northern approach to the bridge as cover. One of the men is getting a haircut. 21st September 1944.

Herbert W. Warhurst, The Times WN5755

BOTTOM LEFT Sappers of 14th Field Squadron Royal Engineers removing German explosives from the road bridge. It had been meticulously prepared for demolition should the need arise but the reason why it was not blown as the Grenadier Guards Shermans drove across remains a mystery. At the last moment a German engineer had pushed the plunger on the detonator box but nothing happened. The most likely reason is that the wires connecting to the detonator had been severed by artillery fire. The alternative and most popular theory is that a young Resistance fighter, Jan van Hoof, cut the wires before he was killed.

Herbert W. Warhurst, The Times WN5753

RIGHT Father Wilhelme Peterse attends to an injured man while the Germans gather up their wounded.
Herbert W. Warhurst, The Times WN5756

TOP LEFT Collaborators are rounded up in Nijmegen.

Herbert W. Warhurst, The Times WN5751

BOTTOM LEFT Men of the 508th Parachute Infantry Regiment stand at an abandoned German position at Beek after an attack on the US 82nd Airborne Division's bridgehead had been repulsed after intense fighting. Note the captured Panzerschreck rocket launcher and ammunition.

Herbert W. Warhurst, The Times WN5772

RIGHT Two men seize the moment to have a wash on a plot of land above Beek. The Stuart tank on the right is from the Nottinghamshire Yeomanry (Sherwood Rangers). This regiment provided armoured support to the US 82nd Airborne during phases of *Market Garden*. The Sherman on the left is an OP tank artillery spotting for the Sexton self-propelled guns of 413th Battery, 147th (Essex Yeomanry) Field Regiment gunners who provided artillery support for the 82nd.

Herbert W. Warhurst, The Times WN5770

LEFT Another missed opportunity associated with *Market Garden* concerned the airstrip at Keent. The 52nd (Lowland) Division could have been flown there in support of the operation but the potential of the airstrip was overlooked until too late in the battle. On 26th September the USAAF's 52nd Troop Carrier Wing flew in the Airborne Forward Delivery Airfield Group to Keent. This image by Bill Tetlow shows C-47s of 37th Squadron of 316 Troop Carrier Group getting close to their destination. They were just some of 209 C-47s that flew in and out during a period of a few hours.

H. William Tetlow, Kemsley M4248G

TOP RIGHT This shot through the windscreen is just as impressive for showing the proximity of the aircraft to each other as 37th Squadron flew in to Keent.

H. William Tetlow, Kemsley M4248G

BOTTOM RIGHT The aim of the game was to get in and out quickly. This C-47 unloads while no fewer than 19 more come into land at short intervals.

H. William Tetlow, Kemsley M4248G

TOP The trip to Keent resulted in several uncharacteristic over-exposures by Bill Tetlow. The changeable autumnal light certainly appears to have been a challenge. This stunning image is worth inclusion for illustrating the scale of the operation.

H. William Tetlow, Kemsley M4248G

BOTTOM Backing a jeep out of a C-47 hold took teamwork. Pioneers and medics from the British 1st Airborne Division were on hand to do the heavy work.

H. William Tetlow, Kemsley M4248G

TOP On 28th September parties of wounded airborne troops from the operation who had been evacuated over the Neder Rijn were flown back to England. Sergeant A. Roscoe of G Squadron, Glider Pilot Regiment, is pictured on the train used to transport the men to hospital on reaching England.

H. William Tetlow, Kemsley M4248F

BOTTOM A tired but dignified Major-General R. E. 'Roy' Urquhart, commander of 1st Airborne, arriving at Cranwell on the 29th. His division was reconstituted in time for him to take it to Norway in May 1945. He went on to be GOC in Malaya during the Emergency before retiring in 1955 having given the army 35 years' devoted service.

Robert Chandler, Kemsley M4248I

Dramatic as events in the Netherlands were, the campaign continued elsewhere. While the Canadians sought to capture the Channel ports German long-range guns continued to bombard Dover. The two shell bursts in this image are real enough but they did not occur at the same time. This 'join up' dated 16th September shows separate incidents from a series of 120 roll films taken from the castle albeit on the same day. In the event this image was not published. *The Times 99648*

LEFT Daily life in the town was constantly disrupted by the threat of shellfire. *The Times* photographer found a number of buses forced to stop in a quiet spot above the town during the bombardment, passengers and crews waiting for things to quieten down before they could continue on their way.

The Times 99666

RIGHT The Germans continued to bombard Dover right until the very end. Calais was liberated on 30th September ending four years of cross-Channel shelling. This image showing damage to a street in Dover was published on 2nd October when news of the cessation of the bombardment was announced in the national press. This is another of the 120 roll images taken by the un-named *The Times* photographer.

The Times 99646

TOP The vast network of caves and tunnels within the white cliffs provided shelter from regular bombardments but casualties were sustained right until the very last. Some of the people shown here also appear on page 109.

Robert Chandler and Herbert Muggeridge, Kemsley M4248L

BOTTOM Dover and the surrounding area had long since earned the name 'Hellfire Corner', but it wasn't all one-way traffic. An array of large-calibre guns were emplaced to fire on German positions and even today a lunar landscape of shell craters can be found on parts of the French coastline beyond Sangatte. Herbert Muggeridge produced a series of images published on 28th September 1944 showing the guns at work. In this image a BL 9.2inch gun at South Foreland Battery opens fire. These guns had a range of around 17 miles (28km) threatening enemy shipping. As Muggeridge was leaving a German shell narrowly missed his car.

Herbert Muggeridge, Kemsley M4248D

TOP A view of Wanstone Battery. The two BL 15inch guns here known as Clem and Jane could fire a shell weighing just under a ton a distance of 23 miles (38km).

Herbert Muggeridge, Kemsley M4248D

BOTTOM A gunner moves one of the huge 15inch shells. The badge on his upper arm is for South-Eastern Command.

Herbert Muggeridge, Kemsley M4248D

TOP This censored image shows women of the Auxiliary Territorial Service working in the combined plotting room.

Herbert Muggeridge, Kemsley M4248D

BOTTOM 'The Mayor of Dover has had official notice that the long-range guns have been captured.' Good news for the embattled citizenry was relayed in all manner of ways.

Herbert Muggeridge, Kemsley M4248L

With the constant shelling stopped at last, it was time for the troglodyte existence of many residents of Dover to come to a much-welcomed end.

Robert Chandler and Herbert Muggeridge, Kemsley M4248L

Herbert Muggeridge and Robert Chandler are pictured at Kemsley House in June 1938. Many of the images they took at Dover have proved impossible to ascribe to either man, so it seems appropriate to use this shot of them together.

Kemsley P1424R

Winter

By late September 1944 the Allied supply situation was under such strain that it became imperative that the approaches to the Scheldt were cleared to open Antwerp. The task fell to the Canadians and they were supported in this task by commando units and other British and Polish formations within the Canadian First Army. Lieutenant-General Harry Crerar's health had deteriorated and his return to Britain for treatment allowed Montgomery to replace him with II Canadian Corps commander Major-General Guy Simonds, in whom he had considerable confidence.

Simonds directed a phased plan to clear the Breskens Pocket, then advance along the corridor of South Beveland and conduct amphibious assaults on fortified Walcheren Island to clear the port of Vlissingen and coastal artillery positions. Only after this was achieved could mines and obstacles be removed from the Scheldt estuary to allow shipping safely into Antwerp.

The operation, known as the battle of the Scheldt, began on 2nd October and would last for a month. Although the Allies were able to employ devastating air power against the Germans, the Canadians had a tough time clearing the Breskens Pocket. After much hard fighting, their efforts allowed the British 52nd (Lowland) Division and supporting commando units to assault the fortified Walcheren Island around the port of Vlissingen (Flushing).

Simonds had identified the need to flood the whole island to trump the German defenders who had flooded part of it themselves to aid their defence. He called in the RAF to breach the dykes and a massive bombing onslaught allowed the sea to pour in. This was followed by an amphibious assault by commandos on Westkapelle and in conjunction with the Canadians advancing doggedly through South Beveland in the face of stiff resistance the Scheldt estuary was gradually cleared. Vlissingen fell on 3rd November and Middleberg, the island's capital, on the 6th. The operation was concluded two days later and engineers began to clear the estuary of obstacles. First Canadian Army had suffered over 12,000 casualties.

With operations to clear the Scheldt taking place at the same time as offensive action elsewhere, Bill Warhurst was a much-travelled man. He crossed into the Netherlands at Putte on 9th October to see the advance on Beveland but broke off from the campaign to record the five-day visit paid by King George VI to his armies in the field. The king made history when he became the first monarch since Henry V to confer knighthoods on the battlefield. Lieutenant-General Miles Dempsey, the commander of Second Army and Lieutenant-General John Crocker, the commander of I British Corps were honoured at an open-air investiture. There was a knighthood, too, for Monty's Chief of Staff, Major-General 'Freddie' de Guingand. Warhurst travelled with the royal party to Verviers across the border into Belgium where the king was welcomed by General Eisenhower and senior American commanders at US First Army Headquarters.

As the King departed for home the war went on. Warhurst followed the advance on s'Hertogenbosch on the 22nd and he was in Tilburg when the town was captured on the 27th. He spent time on South Beveland following the advance to Walcheren where he reached Middleburg as the town fell. He was in Brussels on 9th November for the visit of General Eisenhower and back to the front line as the British pushed on to the Maas and into Germany where he reached Geilenkirchen on 20th November. Some of the heaviest fighting on Dutch soil had taken place as the British bludgeoned their way into Overloon and Venray during Operation *Aintree* before they reached the Maas. Casualties were high, as once again the British infantry bore the brunt.

The last months of 1944 found Bill Tetlow in Paris photographing troops on leave as the city restored itself. There were weddings and parties for orphans and Tetlow even found time to photograph a hair salon for toddlers. Food prices in Paris were of great interest to the *Daily Sketch* as were the availability and cost of women's shoes amongst other things. He attended the trials of collaborators and was on hand to capture Churchill's visit in November where the trip saw a brief return to France by Eric Greenwood.

As Christmas approached Hitler started on his last great gamble in the West, the counter-offensive through the Ardennes, *Unternehmen Wacht am Rhein*, known as the Battle of the Bulge. The aim of the offensive was to reach Antwerp, cut the Allies off from their supply base and split the British and American armies, more or less repeating what happened to the British and French in 1940. Although thrown off balance initially, the Americans quickly recovered and in holding off and then destroying the attackers they inflicted a massive defeat on the Germans, putting an end to any hope of a reversal in the West.

When the Battle of the Bulge began Eisenhower placed the US First and Ninth Armies under Montgomery's direction despite the protests of Omar Bradley. The two US armies cooperated to reduce the northern side of the Bulge while George Patton's Third Army hammered it from the south. Montgomery placed British divisions in positions to free up the Americans to attack the Bulge and extra units were rushed in to assist, including the British 6th Airborne Division.

None of the photographers featured in this book travelled into the American areas to record events from the Bulge. Bill Warhurst confined himself to visits behind the lines filming hospitals and depots full of beer and Christmas goodies. He completely disappears for a whole month leaving radio coverage of Monty's Christmas address and much more besides to Clough and Tetlow. Numbers of 'D-Day men' were given leave over the New Year and the opportunity for positive images of happy soldiers home in England with their loved ones was not to be missed.

By the end of January 1945 Hitler's great gamble had ended in failure for Nazi Germany achieving nothing tangible but further irreparable losses for his armies in the West. If anything the outcome strengthened American resolve in the wake of some infamous excesses by German units and the heroism within pockets of US resistance that achieved something of a mythical status almost immediately. For Monty's armies the Battle of the Bulge represented delays to his plans to advance deeper into the

Reich and for him personally there was further discord with fellow senior commanders. A combination of circumstances, German skulduggery and Monty's knack of ruffling feathers led to a souring of relations between the British and Americans at a crucial time.

For the troops out in the open the weather offered a mix of damp and frosty conditions followed by snow and plummeting temperatures in the New Year. For Dutch civilians in occupied territory things were already at their worst. In September a rail strike had been called by the Dutch government in exile to support the Allied effort to liberate the country and this led to Reichskommissar of the Netherlands, Arthur Seyss-Inquart, and army commander Friedrich Christiansen, ordering a blockade of food supplies to the north-west of the country in retaliation. Thousands died of starvation during the 'Hunger Winter' that followed. Just as resistance in the Reich began to collapse in the final weeks of the war, the Germans allowed the Allies to drop food supplies for the Dutch and relief continued after VE Day. The Dutch imprisoned Christiansen for his actions but like a number of leading Nazis he never completed the full sentence imposed on him. Seyss-Inquart, however, already implicated in genocide, was hanged after Nuremberg.

In January Second Army prepared to clear the Roer Triangle and push into the Reich. Operation *Blackcock* began on 14th January and would last for 12 days. At this stage a pincer movement to trap the Germans west of the Rhine was planned but weather conditions and flooding caused by the Germans hampered movement. The Canadian First Army launched Operation *Veritable* to clear the Reichswald forest on 8th February. At the end of it 50,000 Germans had been taken prisoner at the cost of over 20,000 Anglo-Canadian casualties. The US Ninth Army launched Operation *Grenade* on 9th February but deliberate destruction of dams on the River Roer prevented the Americans from crossing the river until the 23rd. Once across they quickly destroyed German opposition as they advanced to the Rhine.

The British launched Operation *Blockbuster* on 22nd February and the Anglo-Canadians pushed the Germans beyond the Hochwald forest towards Xanten. Despite immense difficulties caused by flooding, the pincer operations had netted around a quarter of a million prisoners. Resistance became increasingly fanatical and the rate of British infantry casualties was a continuous cause for concern. For the Allies the last great obstacle to victory stood in front of them: the River Rhine. Bill Warhurst and the Kemsley photographers were on hand to record these operations. Images showing thousands of German prisoners were a clear signal that victory was getting closer but the awful conditions were also evident.

On 3rd March Churchill came out to Germany and Bill Warhurst filmed his famous visit to the Siegfried Line. The Prime Minister's desire to urinate on the dragon's teeth defences caused him much amusement, but photographers were barred from snapping the exact moment. Churchill was accompanied on his visit by a beaming Field Marshal Alan Brooke who confided in his diary 'I shall never forget the childish grin of intense satisfaction that spread all over his face as he looked down at the critical moment.'

The British had edged up to the western bank of the Rhine at last and the scene was set for the final massive combined offensive of the campaign and the end of the European war.

TOP As if he hadn't been busy enough, the beginning of October would see a month of frantic activity for Bill Warhurst. On the 9th he was in Putte on the Dutch-Belgian border to see the Canadian First Army begin Guy Simonds' plan to clear the Scheldt estuary of German resistance so the port of Antwerp could be opened. These Humber and Daimler armoured cars of the 8th Reconnaissance Regiment (14th Canadian Hussars) of 2nd Canadian Infantry Division appear to be going the wrong way!

Herbert W. Warhurst, The Times WN5789

BOTTOM Three days later HM King George VI arrived in the Netherlands for a five-day visit to 21st Army Group. Some of the best-known images from the royal visit show Monty briefing the king in his map caravan. This is one of two frames taken by Bill Warhurst.

Herbert W. Warhurst, The Times WN5815

TOP The king carried out a series of investitures. Here we see Major-General Guy Simonds taking leave from his campaign to clear the Scheldt to be honoured as a Companion of the Most Honourable Order of the Bath, a chivalric order founded by King George I.

Herbert W. Warhurst, The Times WN5816

BOTTOM The negative showing the king and Simonds was cropped for publication purposes by having black paper fixed across the glass. The resultant image would need further close cropping to be of any use.

Author

TOP This image was taken at the Taenakker monastery where the king met officers of the US 82nd Airborne Division, introduced by Brigadier-General James M Gavin. XXX Corps commander Lieutenant-General Brian Horrocks looks on. The five officers in the line-up are, left to right; Colonel F. Andrew March III, 320th Glider Field Artillery Battalion; Colonel Roy E. Linquist, 508th Parachute Infantry Regiment, Colonel Reuben H. Tucker, 504th Parachute Infantry Regiment, Colonel William E. Eckman, 505th Parachute Infantry Regiment and Lieutenant Colonel Charles W. Billingslea, 325th Glider Infantry Regiment.

Herbert W. Warhurst, The Times WN5813.

BOTTOM On the next day the king travelled to Belgium to meet General Eisenhower at the US First Army headquarters at Verviers. There is a well-known image of the king sharing a joke with Ike while Bradley and Hodges look on. This shot, complete with cropping marks painted on to the emulsion, was taken slightly earlier.

Herbert W. Warhurst, The Times WN5824

Ike gathered his generals for a group photograph. Of Bill Warhurst's two frames this first one of the generals sorting themselves out is the nicest. *Front row L–R*: Lieutenant General-George S. Patton Jnr, US Third Army; Lieutenant-General Omar N. Bradley, US Twelfth Army Group; General Dwight D. Eisenhower, Supreme Commander Allied Expeditionary Force; Lieutenant-General Courtney H. Hodges, US First Army; Lieutenant-General William H. Simpson, US Ninth Army. *Middle row L–R*: Major-General William B. Kean, Chief-of-Staff US First Army; Major-General Charles E. Corlett, US XIX Corps; Major-General J. Lawton Collins, US VII Corps; Major-General Leonard T. Gerow, US V Corps; Major-General Elwood R. 'Pete' Quesada, IX Tactical Air Command. *Back row L–R*: Major-General Leven C. Allen, Chief-of-Staff US Twelfth Army Group; Brigadier-General Charles E. Hart, artillery commander US First Army; and Brigadier-General Truman C. Thorson, General Staff Operations US First Army.

Herbert W. Warhurst, The Times WN5826

TOP LEFT On the last day King George VI became the first British monarch to confer a knighthood on the battlefield since King Henry V at Agincourt in 1415. Perhaps more significantly he enjoys the distinction of being the last British monarch to fight in a battle; he was stationed in a turret aboard the battleship HMS *Collingwood* at Jutland in May 1916. Miles Dempsey and John Crocker were also knighted in the field at Eindhoven by the king; but the inclusion of Monty's Chief of Staff Major-General Francis 'Freddie' De Guingand, seen here, was the most unusual. He was still only a substantive major at the time but his brilliance was never in doubt. Monty's faithful servant, Sergeant Norman Kirby, borrowed the stool from a local church and the cushion for the regalia held by the king's equerry was made using an evening dress provided by a local lady.
Herbert W. Warhurst, The Times WN5832

BOTTOM LEFT At the end of proceedings various people were introduced to the king including Bill Warhurst, standing second from right in this image by an unknown photographer.
The Times WN7010A

RIGHT The war went on. Local lads find a good spot to watch events in a classically Dutch landscape. The marching troops are from 2nd Battalion Glasgow Highlanders, 46th (Highland) Infantry Brigade. *Herbert W. Warhurst, The Times WN5843*

LEFT As the battle of the Scheldt raged on, Monty's armies drove deep into the Netherlands to protect the flank of the forces fighting their way along South Beveland. At the same time the British pushed out towards the Maas and the costly battle of Overloon would see much death and destruction before the devastated village and nearby Venray fell to British troops by 18th October. By this time Bill Warhurst had been joined in the Netherlands by R. H. Clough of Kemsley Newspapers and they often covered the same ground. Sadly, no employment records relating to Clough or images of him remain in the News UK archive and, like Frederick Skinner, his name disappears from the Kemsley negative diaries after the war. This print image shows troops hunting down snipers in Overloon.

R. H. Clough, Kemsley M4248Z

TOP RIGHT While he was at the front line near Venray, R. H. Clough was asked to produce a series of images showing British troops 'in action' for use in Kemsley titles. This shot of a QF 17-pounder anti-tank gun has a greater deal of authenticity than many of the others.

R. H. Clough, Kemsley M4251Q

BOTTOM RIGHT The headlong advance across northern France and Belgium had been known as 'the swan' by British troops but the Netherlands proved to be an unforgiving battlefield and the intense fighting endured thus far was set to get worse. The censor would not approve photographs of British dead for publication, so this image taken at Puttershoek near Nuland showing two tanks that had fallen victim to mines during the advance on s'Hertogenbosch is unlikely to have been seen by many people. The Cromwell has been wrecked while the second tank suffered an internal explosion throwing sections of the hull in all directions.

Herbert W. Warhurst, The Times WN5857A

TOP LEFT Warhurst's image of the Army Catering Corps at work shows an important aspect of life on the road with Second Army. Although popularly attributed to Napoleon, the saying 'An army marches on its stomach' may also be claimed by Frederick the Great or even Claudius Galen, chief physician to the Roman legions. Whoever said it, Private E. Barker from Ely in Cambridgeshire found a ready audience while baking apple dumplings for the gunners of 323rd Battery, 81st (Glamorgan Yeomanry) Field Regiment.

Herbert W. Warhurst, The Times WN5862

BOTTOM LEFT The crews of these Churchill tanks of 141st Regiment (The Buffs) Royal Armoured Corps have stopped for lunch on the road near Wijbosch. This unit was equipped with Crocodile flamethrower tanks, a fearsome weapon the Germans came to hate with good cause.

Herbert W. Warhurst, The Times WN5874

RIGHT The drive towards s'Hertogenbosch reaped unexpected benefits. When Schijndel was taken on the 23rd a party of American airborne troops stranded since *Market Garden* were able to emerge from hiding at Sint Lidwina Maternity Hospital. The Americans were sheltered by members of the Dutch Resistance, three of whom – Cor Laanen, Christ van Bakel and Gree Scholten – were pictured with the men when Bill Warhurst arrived at the hospital.

Herbert W. Warhurst, The Times WN5866

LEFT s'Hertogenbosch fell to the 53rd (Welsh) Infantry Division on 26th October 1944. Here divisional commander Major-General R. K. 'Bobby' Ross directs operations in a suburb of the town from his Humber Light Reconnaissance Car.

Herbert W. Warhurst, The Times WN5997

TOP RIGHT On the same day Canadian anti-tank gunners found themselves at the gates of Camp Vught better known to the Nazis as Konzentrationslager Herzogenbusch. It was one of two concentration camps run by the SS in occupied Western Europe, the other being at Natzweiler in France. Vught housed over 30,000 inmates, nearly all of them transferred to camps in the east a short time before the Allies arrived. R. H. Clough elected not to photograph anything particularly unpleasant, choosing instead to concentrate on details. His caption claims 13,000 people died at the camp but while this may be an exaggeration this book really is no place for semantics. This image shows one of three ovens used to cremate victims of Nazi brutality at the site.

R. H. Clough, Kemsley M4248H

BOTTOM RIGHT Camp Vught was the centre of several work groups operating for the financial gain of the SS. Inmates seconded to the Luftwaffe-Kommando were used to strip crashed German and Allied aircraft and conditions for them were very harsh. The remains of several aircraft were on site when the Allies arrived including a B-24 Liberator.

R. H. Clough, Kemsley M4248H

By the end of November the Allies were using Camp Vught to house homeless Germans swept up in the advance and the camp was also used to intern members of the Dutch SS, their families and other collaborators.

R. H. Clough, Kemsley M4251Q

British heavy artillery firing in support of the advance on Tilburg: a development of obsolete Great War-era guns, these BL 7.2inch howitzers could lob a 200lb shell just under 10 miles but the recoil was brutal creating the need for ramps to catch the gun as it leaped back. There were occasions when the recoiling gun would actually clear the ramps so gunners quickly learned to keep a judicious distance from the trail when firing.

Herbert W. Warhurst, The Times WN5998

By the next day Bill Warhurst had headed west into the First Canadian Army area of operations to witness the fall of Tilburg to the 15th (Scottish) Division. Getting into the town was no small task with an abundance of waterways creating many obstacles. A bridge has been laid across a canal allowing armour to drive into the town. Ram Kangaroo armoured personnel carriers and men of the Gordon Highlanders sporting flowers on their helmets ride into Tilburg while work to finish the bridge goes on. A 79th Armoured Division Churchill AVRE and a Caterpillar armoured bulldozer complete the scene. The Kangaroo was a Canadian innovation that was quickly copied by the Allies often by stripping weapons from self-propelled guns or converting obsolete tanks. In this case unwanted Canadian Ram tanks had their turrets removed to create room for twelve infantrymen. The Kangaroo would save many an infantryman's life in the months to come. The 1st Canadian Armoured Personnel Carrier Regiment operated the vehicles. It was the only Canadian regiment to be formed and disbanded overseas without ever serving at home.

Herbert W. Warhurst, The Times WN6006

LEFT The capture of Tilburg on 27th October secured the right flank of the units fighting to clear the Scheldt where intense fighting was hampered by dreadful conditions. The people of Tilburg gave 15th (Scottish) Division a rapturous welcome.

R. H. Clough, Kemsley M4251Q

TOP RIGHT The commander of 15th (Scottish) Division was Major-General Colin Barber, who at 6 feet 9 inches tall had the obvious nickname 'Tiny'. He is pictured with the Burgomaster of Tilburg Jan Christiaan van de Mortel who had worked tirelessly against the German occupation and been imprisoned for his efforts.

Herbert W. Warhurst, The Times WN6010

BOTTOM RIGHT As with so many liberated communities recriminations against collaborators began almost immediately.

R. H. Clough, Kemsley M4274W

Men of 52nd (Lowland) Division crossing onto a bleak Walcheren on what appears to be a bright day. German prisoners help carry back the wounded.

Herbert W. Warhurst, The Times WN6027

TOP LEFT Women wearing traditional dress complete with *kissers* attached to their turbans help men of the Cameronians cook a meal at s'Heer-Arendskerke on South Beveland.

Herbert W. Warhurst, The Times WN6040

BOTTOM LEFT German resistance on Walcheren ended with the fall of the capital Middleburg on 6th November 1944. This well-known image shows the senior German officer, General Wilhelm Daser commanding 70.Infanterie-Division after he had formally surrendered to Major R. H. B. Johnston of the Royal Scots. Johnston had promoted himself to 'colonel' to satisfy Daser's wish to treat with a senior officer. This image is often captioned as showing Johnston with Daser, but the man on the left is a sapper officer escorting the general into captivity. The 70th had put up a good fight belying their status as a static formation known as a 'white bread' or 'stomach' division made up of men with delicate constitutions.

Herbert W. Warhurst, The Times WN6045

RIGHT The end on Walcheren: Germans queuing up to go into captivity are the object of curiosity for people of all ages.

Herbert Warhurst, The Times WN6055

TOP LEFT Bill Tetlow arrived in Paris while fighting raged in the Netherlands. After four years of occupation the city was rediscovering its sense of style and it proved to be fertile territory for Bill Tetlow's camera. Paris was a magnet for people on leave and in the wake of the *Liberation* it had become home to a number of Allied military and civilian organisations. But there was serious business to attend to and the trials of *collabos* who had served Vichy and the Nazis were under way. There is something almost surreal about this image of the journalist and biographer Georges Suarez in discussion with his counsel on 23rd October 1944, the day he was sentenced to death for his support for the Vichy regime.

H. William Tetlow, Kemsley M4248Z.

BOTTOM LEFT A partisan crowd attended the court expecting to see justice done. In his defence Suarez declared that he 'wished to serve France' but according to contemporary reports this was greeted with strong indignation in the packed courtroom.

H. William Tetlow, Kemsley M4248Z

RIGHT Suarez stands in the dock to hear his fate. The *Daily Sketch* summed up its feelings succinctly. 'He sold his pen to the Nazis and, by his own writings, was proved a traitor.' Court President Leroux told him 'During four years of occupation you never ceased to collaborate, reserving your sarcasms and insults for those who resisted.' Fifty-four-year-old Suarez was executed by firing squad in November 1944.

H. William Tetlow, Kemsley M4248Z

WINTER **135**

LEFT If the use of a pen in support of the Nazis was enough to get a man shot then the murder of a patriot who stood up to the Germans was another matter altogether. Factions within the Vichy regime were itching for revenge following the murder of Information Minister Philippe Henriot and the Nazis were happy to supply a victim in the form of Georges Mandel, a pre-war minister. Mandel had taken an uncompromising stance against the Vichy regime and the decision to kill him was expedited by members of the Milice assisted by the Gestapo. Brought to Paris on a pretext, his car was diverted into the woods of Fontainebleau on 7th July where the Milicien Jean Mansuy fired 14 rounds at him from close range. Mandel suspected he was being set up for assassination because he told Milice official Max Knipping 'To die is nothing. What is sad is to die without seeing the liberation of the country and the restoration of the Republic.' Mansuy and his accomplices claimed the Resistance had ambushed them, but other players in the saga were not so careful with their stories. Mansuy was shot 'trying to escape' after failing to pass himself off as a *Resistant* on 25th August, the day of the *Liberation* when he may have been attempting to kill Charles de Gaulle. His Milicien accomplices Georges Néroni, Pierre Boéro and Pierre Lambert are seen in the dock during a speedy trial on 25th October. Néroni and Boéro were executed in November but Lambert, a bit part player, was sentenced to 20 years' hard labour.

H. William Tetlow, Kemsley M4251Q

TOP RIGHT Winston Churchill arrived in Paris on 11th November to commemorate Armistice Day and received a magnificent welcome. His relationship with General Charles de Gaulle had always been difficult to say the least but unlike Roosevelt he had recognised that the general offered the best hope to lead the Free French against the Nazis and their Vichy puppets and to rejuvenate the country once it had been liberated. Charles de Gaulle's distrust of 'les Anglo-Saxons' was as strong as his determination to see liberated France take her place on the world stage once more. He held a grudging respect for Churchill because he had stuck by him and any differences the men had were set aside during the visit. Churchill inspects the guard of honour on arrival at Orly. His long-held admiration for the French Army seems evident in this image.

Eric Greenwood, The Times DD455

BOTTOM RIGHT Churchill and de Gaulle lay wreaths at the Arc de Triomphe.

Eric Greenwood, The Times DD444

LEFT Both men received the adulation of the huge crowd on the Champs Élysée. These images are very atmospheric but show the limitations of using plate cameras during fast-moving situations.

Eric Greenwood, The Times DD447

RIGHT Bill Tetlow found things just as awkward from his vantage point.
H. William Tetlow, Kemsley M4251Q.

LEFT At the front, Second Army were advancing on Venlo and Roermond. Crossing the Maas would see them ever closer to German soil. These tanks of 33rd Armoured Brigade make for an interesting procession as they cross the canal at Nederweert on 15th November 1944. The first two are Sherman I Hybrid variants of 1st Northamptonshire Yeomanry.

Herbert W. Warhurst, The Times WN6078

TOP RIGHT A soldier displays a Schu-mine 42 for Bill Warhurst's camera. These little anti-personnel mines had 7oz of explosive (200g) in a wooden container and hardly any metal components making them very difficult to detect with the technology available. While a mine like this could be lethal, injuries to lower limbs were more prevalent for anyone having the misfortune to detonate one. Mines and booby-traps in all shapes and sizes were sown in large numbers by the retreating Germans.

Herbert W. Warhurst, The Times WN6075

BOTTOM RIGHT A day later Warhurst was at Heythuysen edging ever closer to the Maas where he snapped three war correspondents checking their map. The man named in the centre is the Australian Ronnie Monson of the Sydney *Daily Telegraph*. He was a much-travelled and veteran correspondent of conflict in China and Spain who had witnessed the Blitzkrieg in 1940 and been Mentioned in Despatches when he saved the life of a soldier during the revolt in Iraq in 1941. After the Second World War he covered conflicts in the Middle East and Korea. He died in 1973. The slogan on the house reads 'We will never capitulate'. The increasingly fanatical nature of the German defence had its roots in the Allied demand for unconditional surrender by the Nazis. Many felt they had nothing to lose and fought to the bitter end because the Allies left no room for manoeuvre at the negotiating table.

Herbert W. Warhurst, The Times WN6089

THE LIBERATION OF EUROPE 1944–1945

Armies in retreat have been destroying bridges since time immemorial and the Germans were no different. While no location or date is given, this railway bridge on the Maas offers a typical scene of destruction.

R. H. Clough M4253N

Bofors anti-aircraft gunners 'in the Maas sector' welcome the dawn of another day.

R. H. Clough, Kemsley M4256J

Into the Reich: 18th November 1944. Machine gunners of 1st Motor Battalion Grenadier Guards fire on German positions on the road to Geilenkirchen. Experience from the Great War had shown the devastating impact batteries of Vickers machine guns could have in the indirect fire role pouring down thousands of rounds on troop concentrations or defensive positions without having a direct line of sight. Mounting the guns on a Universal Carrier to create the Carrier MMG was a logical progression.

Herbert W. Warhurst, The Times WN6104

BOTTOM LEFT Later that day Bill photographed 12 Shermans placed track to track bombarding the enemy from their position on the Gangelt–Geilenkirchen road.

Herbert W. Warhurst, The Times WN6110

TOP General Dwight D. Eisenhower arrived at Monty's headquarters at Zonhoven on 29th November creating photo opportunities. Here the two men enjoy a quiet chat in cosy surroundings betraying little of their at times difficult relationship.

Herbert W. Warhurst, The Times WN6154

BOTTOM Happily, Bill Warhurst took a moment to photograph a group of Monty's staff. *L–R*: Captain Ray BonDurrant, Captain Noel Chavasse, Lieutenant Colonel Trumbull Warren, Lieutenant Colonel Kit Dawnay and Captain Johnny Henderson.

Herbert W. Warhurst, The Times WN6155

TOP With the season of goodwill close at hand, patients and nursing staff put up Christmas decorations at the 79th British General Hospital at Eindhoven on 4th December 1944.

Herbert W. Warhurst, The Times WN6171

BOTTOM Dutch kids enjoying British Army-issue tea and sandwiches on St Nicholas Day, somewhere near Eindhoven, 6th December 1944.

Herbert W. Warhurst, The Times WN6180

LEFT The shops of Paris were all ready for Christmas.
H. William Tetlow, Kemsley M42530

TOP RIGHT Meanwhile British troops in Brussels were busy buying presents for their loved ones.
Herbert W. Warhurst, The Times WN6209

BOTTOM RIGHT Cheerful local helpers assisted with Second Army's Christmas mail deliveries.
Herbert W. Warhurst, The Times WN6194

LEFT Corporal Eric Matthews of Neath gives out sweets and chocolate to Parisian orphans at a Christmas party given by SHAEF.
H. William Tetlow, Kemsley M4256J

RIGHT This mountain of Guinness stout and Bass ale was being readied for distribution through the NAAFI on 14th December. Two days later *Unternehmen Wacht am Rhein* – the German counter-offensive known as the Battle of the Bulge – began. It was the last throw of the dice by Hitler in the West and it ended in defeat for his armies. The Bulge delayed Monty's plans for clearing the Reichswald Forest and the Roer Triangle and forced his armies on the defensive over Christmas and into the New Year. Bill Warhurst went on leave during this period and his negatives diary plays catch up listing several jobs including images we have already seen of Dirk Bogarde and Bob Cooper. His last job in 1944 shows this warehouse full of beer and it would be a month before he sent anything new.

Herbert W. Warhurst, The Times WN6217

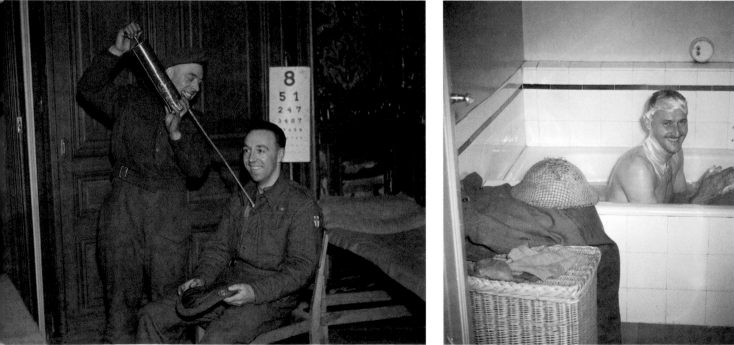

THE LIBERATION OF EUROPE 1944–1945

TOP LEFT Kemsley photographers remained busy. This image shows a leave ballot in progress. The luck of the draw could mean precious time at home in the UK. Sergeant Stevens of Hanwell is about to get lucky.

R. H. Clough, Kemsley M4256J

BOTTOM LEFT Having had a medical to ensure he is fit enough for leave, Sapper J. F. Sawyer of Walthamstow puts on a brave face as he is fumigated.

R. H. Clough, Kemsley M4256J

BOTTOM MIDDLE It is hard to imagine what the luxury of a hot bath felt like after so long, even with a newspaper photographer on hand to record the experience. Sapper Tom Barnaby is all smiles regardless of the attention.

H. William Tetlow, Kemsley M4251Q

TOP RIGHT There were other delights. A leave party arrive at their accommodation in Paris. Most of these men appear to be sappers and the disparity between ages is quite apparent.

H. William Tetlow, Kemsley M42451Q

TOP LEFT The leave ballot meant some D-Day veterans were able to get home for a few days. One of them was Lance Corporal Charles Woodgate of Willesden in north-west London who arrived home on New Year's Day. Sidney Beadell followed some of his time at home including a family outing to see a pantomime on 2nd January. The Woodgates are pictured with their children Alma, Donald and baby Alan.

Sidney Beadell, Kemsley M4254W

BOTTOM LEFT Paris undoubtedly had its attractions. Here Signaller Storman chats up a couple of local ladies on the steps of the opera house while his mates, Signallers Tebbs, Hancock and Pollock look on.

H. William Tetlow, Kemsley M4251Q

RIGHT Quite a number of women in uniform were also hoping to enjoy the magic of the 'City of Light'. It would be interesting to know what these two WAAFs thought of some of the sights they saw in the city.

H. William Tetlow, Kemsley M4274W

LEFT Those front-line troops unfortunate not to get leave remained on duty, often in miserable circumstances. 'The island', a 3-mile-long rectangle of inundated land between the Waal and the Neder Rijn has been prominent in recent years thanks to works such as Stephen E. Ambrose's *Band of Brothers*. After the failure of *Market Garden* it formed an inhospitable swamp between the Allied and German lines and it became a lethal strip where regular artillery duels and clashes between patrols took place amid awful conditions. R. H. Clough took a series of images there but the light defeated him. This image of British troops patrolling by boat on 14th December 1944 is one of the usable shots.

R. H. Clough, Kemsley M4256J

RIGHT A Bren gunner keeping watch from a ruined farm building on the same day.

R. H. Clough, Kemsley M4256J

LEFT On 17th December – the second day of the German counter-offensive in the Ardennes, Monty recorded his Christmas message to 21st Army Group for broadcast by the BBC. There was a carol concert and he appears to have joined in with a minimum of enthusiasm, his mind on serious matters elsewhere. Monty's address was printed for distribution throughout his armies and was repeated in *The Times*. He told them 'Last Christmas we were in England, expectant and full of hope; this Christmas we are fighting in Germany. The conquest of Germany remains… Therefore, with faith in God, and with enthusiasm for our cause and for the day of battle, let us continue the contest with stout hearts and with determination to conquer.'

R. H. Clough, Kemsley M4253N

RIGHT Less than a year on from the famous group photograph of the senior invasion leaders at Norfolk House we saw at the beginning of the book, two of the men pictured were dead. Trafford Leigh-Mallory's Avro York flew into a French mountainside on his way out to Ceylon (Sri Lanka) on 14th November. Another air crash in France robbed Britain and the Allies of one of the great figures of the war when Admiral Sir Bertram Ramsay's Lockheed Hudson crashed on take-off at Toussus-le-Noble on 2nd January 1945. Like Nelson, he died on the cusp of a famous victory. The planner of the Dunkirk evacuation of 1940 and the Sicilian and Normandy landings, his loss was keenly felt. Senior Allied commanders attended the funeral at Saint-Germain-en-Laye but even this occasion was subject to the attentions of the censor.

H. William Tetlow, Kemsley M4256J

LEFT A group of lads find a novel playground for a snowball fight in Paris. The Panther may well be one of a number lost in the city back in August by the Germans.

H. William Tetlow, Kemsley M4256J

TOP RIGHT Just as the weather deteriorated Bill Tetlow left Paris on his way to the front line in the Netherlands. He paid a visit to a Mixed Anti-Aircraft battery on 13th January 1945 where he photographed women of the ATS operating rangefinders and predictors for 3.7inch guns. Although mixed units met with approval women were barred from working the guns. There do not appear to have been any issues about them getting their tot of the rum ration. It was delivered in the same type of SD jar men of the Great War would recognise.

H. William Tetlow, Kemsley M4256P

BOTTOM RIGHT Twin sisters Muriel and Beryl Smith of Didsbury, Manchester, seem happy to be out of the snow.

H. William Tetlow, Kemsley M4256P

TOP LEFT While the Allies faced fanatical resistance during their advance into Germany there were other places where Germans were prepared to hold out until the bitter end. The garrisons of St Nazaire, La Rochelle and Royan on the Atlantic coast obeyed Hitler's demand that they never surrender. For the French, subduing these places took on great significance and with American support they lay siege and attempted to prise the enemy out but the Germans would not budge. With a large civilian population on their hands in St Nazaire since early autumn the Germans happily agreed to a succession of ceasefires beginning 16th January 1945 to allow people to leave for nearby Nantes. The German and Franco-American negotiators met at the battered railway station at Cordemais on the perimeter of German-held territory to agree terms for trains to pass across the lines. They were accompanied by a number of Allied journalists, one of whom was Kemsley photographer Frederick Skinner. A jovial Hauptmann Muller, the German chief negotiator, points out that time is of the essence. The smiling Luftwaffe officer to his left is Oberleutnant Dietrich Schulz-Köhn, a leading light in the German jazz music movement despite Nazi disapproval of the genre. During the occupation of Paris he remained friends with a number of musicians whose ethnicity made them targets for the Nazis including the great Django Reinhardt. After the war he became a successful broadcaster under the name 'Dr Jazz' and was honoured for his contribution to German culture. He died in 1999.
Frederick R. Skinner, Kemsley M4256P

TOP MIDDLE Skinner's caption claims there were 1,200 people on board the first train out of St Nazaire while other reports claim 750. Around 10,000 people eventually left the port. A smiling Hauptmann Muller observes events while relieved evacuees look on. This appears to have been taken during a later ceasefire because the snow has gone.
Frederick R. Skinner, Kemsley E7366

TOP RIGHT The German garrison did not surrender until 11th May 1945. These French troops besieging the port are typical of the period after General de Gaulle had ordered the absorption of FFI units into the French Army. These men wear pre-1940 French uniform and have German rifles.
Frederick R. Skinner, Kemsley M4256P

LEFT Frederick Skinner was photographed chatting with Hauptmann Muller and other press correspondents. He requested that copies of pictures of him be sent home to his wife in Southport.
Kemsley M4256P

LEFT Second Army launched Operation *Blackcock* to reduce the Roer Triangle on 14th January with the aim of pushing the Germans over their frontier. Fighting was fierce causing considerable damage to villages on both sides of the border. At Schilberg, smiling tank crewmen wearing Pixie over-suits point the way to Germany on the 19th. The slogan on the wall reads 'On to Victory with the Führer!'

Herbert W. Warhurst, The Times WN6244

RIGHT The crew of this wrecked Churchill Crocodile will have had much less to smile about.
Herbert W. Warhurst, The Times WN6242

TOP LEFT Bill Tetlow wrote that he didn't see a single undamaged building in the border town of Höngen following its capture on 20th January. Here a Churchill Crocodile of 141st Regiment (The Buffs) of the Royal Armoured Corps leads the way past a couple of unwarlike Dennis tipper lorries.

H. William Tetlow, Kemsley M4274W

BOTTOM LEFT By 23rd January Bill Warhurst had begun crossing paths with the 8th King's Royal Irish Hussars on the way to victory. This image shows two officers who did not survive the war. Twenty-three-year-old Lieutenant John Pim of Rathdowney in Ireland was killed on 8th April. Twenty-two-year-old Lieutenant Walter Ryde of Bournemouth was killed on the 20th of that month. They are pictured with a German patrol dog they picked up near Sint Joost.

Herbert W. Warhurst, The Times WN6276

TOP RIGHT The latest advance into Germany by Second Army achieved all its objectives. This recce party are riding in a carrier near Pütt, south-west of Heinsberg.

Herbert W. Warhurst, The Times WN6281

BOTTOM RIGHT But the advance was never without cost. This burning Churchill fell victim to a mine near Laffeld. Crew members beat a hasty retreat with recovered items.

H. William Tetlow, Kemsley M4256P (print)

TOP LEFT Infantrymen take a breather as a Sherman Crab flail tank moves down an icy track.

H. William Tetlow E6591 (print)

BOTTOM LEFT The superior quality of German armoured vehicles was appreciated all too well by the Allies and there were many examples of captured equipment being put into service. This Panther Ausf G named *Cuckoo* was captured by 4th Tank Battalion Coldstream Guards near Overloon in October 1944 and did good work until the troublesome fuel pump caused an engine fire destroying the vehicle. It is pictured on 26th January.

Herbert W. Warhurst, The Times WN6294

RIGHT Troops work their way through a landscape resonant of winters during the Great War as they advance on Heinsberg.
H. William Tetlow, Kemsley M4256P

TOP LEFT The heaviest gun in the arsenal of Second Army was the American-built 240mm Howitzer M1 operated, here, by 3rd Super Heavy Regiment Royal Artillery. The huge gun could lob a 300lb shell just over 14 miles and needed a crew of 14 to operate it. A good number of them were required to ram the shell home. Note the gunner carrying the bag of propellant charge. The gun was named the Black Dragon in US service, but Bill Warhurst tells us this one was known much less prosaically as 'The Slogger'.

Herbert W. Warhurst, The Times WN6306

BOTTOM LEFT Gunner H. Ginns of Desborough in Northamptonshire sets the fuse on one of the massive shells.

Herbert W. Warhurst, The Times WN6296

RIGHT Sergeant J. W. Wilson of Peterhead inspects the breach.

Herbert W. Warhurst, The Times WN6298

TOP LEFT The next phase of Monty's plan saw the launch of Operation *Veritable*, a month-long campaign aimed at clearing the Germans out of the Reichswald Forest, pushing them back towards Xanten. Bill Warhurst spent much of his time in the operational area of the Canadian First Army. As was often the case, he concentrated on photographing the British units within it. This image shows troops waiting to advance into the forest near the village of Bruuk on the Dutch–German frontier on 9th February 1945.

Herbert W. Warhurst, The Times WN6323

BOTTOM LEFT Bill Tetlow was in Gennep on the eastern bank of the Maas as British troops dealt with snipers on 11th February.

H. William Tetlow, Kemsley (un-numbered print)

RIGHT A brief halt at Nutterden.

Herbert W. Warhurst, The Times WN6340

TOP LEFT Street fighting in Kleve. Bill Warhurst followed tanks and men of the Gordon Highlanders clearing out snipers where 'quite a few were taken out'. He refers to the town's history as the birthplace of Anne of Cleves, fourth wife of King Henry VIII in his caption. Wagner's *Lohengrin* and its connection to the legend of the Knight of the Swan was also on his mind.

Herbert W. Warhurst, The Times WN6353

MIDDLE LEFT A suspected sniper is rounded up in Kleve.

Herbert W. Warhurst, The Times WN6363

BOTTOM LEFT The quagmire on forest tracks was a challenge for the units of the Guards Armoured Division advancing into the Reichswald. The driver of this jeep seems fairly relaxed despite the difficulties.

Herbert W. Warhurst, The Times WN6370

RIGHT The advancing British were far from out of the woods when they encountered inundated areas along the Lower Rhine. This motorcyclist is a picture of concentration on the treacherous road.

Herbert W. Warhurst, The Times WN6377

LEFT 'Water, water everywhere…'
Herbert W. Warhurst, The Times WN6381

TOP RIGHT The amphibious LVT Buffalo was indispensable. A fully laden Universal Carrier just about fits on board.
Herbert W. Warhurst, The Times WN6366

BOTTOM RIGHT Bill Tetlow's caption for this image claims this is an overturned German tank, but it is, in fact, a Churchill. A military policeman on traffic duty has propped his motorcycle up against it.
H. William Tetlow, Kemsley E6671

LEFT Tetlow also photographed this wrecked railway siding where a number of 79th Armoured Division Churchill AVRE tanks have been gathered. No caption survives and this unnumbered image was 'killed' by the censor because these tanks may well be battle damaged. The glass negative itself has two parts snapped off, but fortunately the main area is fine.

H. William Tetlow, Kemsley (unnumbered negative)

TOP RIGHT There were other perils to beware of. Men from a Royal Engineers bomb disposal unit deal with an unexploded 1,000lb bomb at Goch, which was in Allied hands on 21st February.

Herbert W. Warhurst, The Times WN6416

BOTTOM RIGHT Troops also had to be on the lookout for VIPs. Here Monty and Lieutenant-General Brian Horrocks chat to a sergeant of 79th (The Scottish Horse) Medium Regiment while they toured the area handing out newspapers and cigarettes.

Herbert W. Warhurst, The Times WN6424

LEFT The twin towers of the magnificent St Laurentius church in Uedem, which was completed in 1886, survived the assault on the town; but the rest of the building was totally destroyed. A new church opened in 1960.

Herbert W. Warhurst, The Times WN6443

RIGHT British troops and armour amid the ruins of Uedem. The launch of Operation *Blockbuster* on 22nd February brought about a successful conclusion to *Veritable*, which had seen over 20,000 Germans taken prisoner with as many again killed or seriously wounded. *Veritable* had been planned as part of a pincer movement in conjunction with the US Ninth Army's Operation *Grenade* but the Germans had destroyed dams on the Roer and Lieutenant-General William H. Simpson's troops could not cross the river until flood waters had subsided on the 23rd. Once across, however, the pincer movement was a great success. Hitler's disastrous order that divisions west of the Rhine should stand and fight saw over a quarter of a million men taken prisoner as the Allies progressed.

Herbert W. Warhurst, The Times WN6450

LEFT 'A German paratrooper pays the price – trying to stem our advance', 28th February 1945. This close-up showing the grim reality of Hitler's strategy was taken on the outskirts of Kalkar.

Herbert W. Warhurst, The Times WN6458

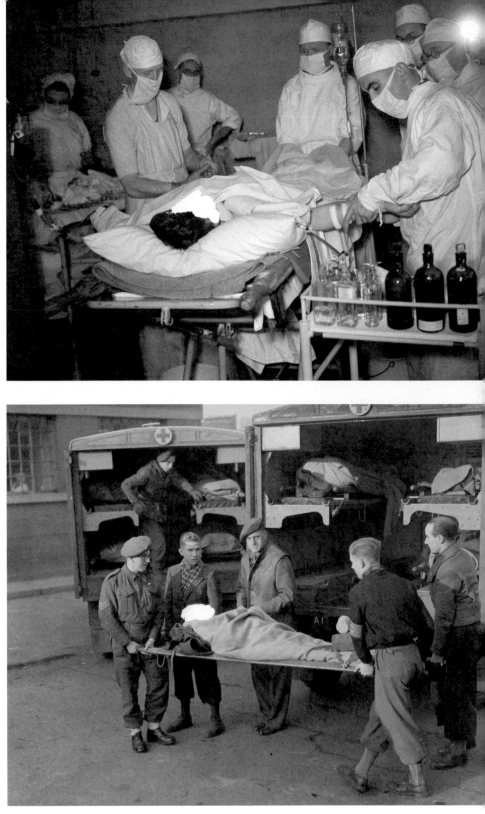

TOP RIGHT *Veritable, Grenade* and *Blockbuster* inflicted over 20,000 casualties on the Allied armies involved. Bill Tetlow visited a British forward hospital in Belgium, but there are no details of where this was. The censor has ordered the face of this soldier having surgery to be painted out.

H. William Tetlow M4267X

BOTTOM RIGHT More casualties arrive and, again, the censor has required faces of the wounded to be obscured. According to Tetlow's caption 'young Belgian boys assist the hard-pressed hospital staff by acting as stretcher-bearers.'

H. William Tetlow M4267X

THE LIBERATION OF EUROPE 1944–1945

TOP LEFT On 1st March General Eisenhower visited Monty's headquarters at Geldrop to award medals to a number of officers. It was an opportunity for a photo call showing the unity of the Allied command following the tensions arising from the Battle of the Bulge and much more besides. This image is a model of decorum as Monty, Ike and Bradley have a friendly chat. Eisenhower had deservedly been promoted to the five-star rank of General of the Army on 20th December 1944 restoring parity with Montgomery.

Herbert W. Warhurst, The Times WN6466

BOTTOM LEFT Two days later Winston Churchill achieved his ambition to pee on the Siegfried Line to show his utter contempt for Hitler and the Third Reich. Field Marshal Sir Alan Brooke accompanied Churchill and noted his obvious pleasure. US Ninth Army commander Lieutenant-General William H. Simpson and Monty complete the line up in this image. No photographs of Churchill enjoying his high jinks were permitted, but there are a number showing the PM and his companions amid the dragon's teeth of the West Wall.

Herbert W. Warhurst, The Times WN6480

RIGHT Simpson briefs Churchill and Monty as Brooke looks on.

Herbert W. Warhurst, The Times WN6483

TOP The British were near the Rhine when Bill Warhurst took this image of men from 15th/19th King's Royal Hussars, the armoured reconnaissance regiment of 11th Armoured Division, who knocked out this Jagdpanzer IV L/70. They are taking a closer look at their handiwork near Xanten on 11th March 1945.

Herbert W. Warhurst, The Times WN6510

BOTTOM Wash day had arrived at last nearly six years after Jimmy Kennedy had written the popular wartime song *We're Going to Hang Out the Washing on the Siegfried Line* in 1939 while stationed in France with the BEF.

Herbert W. Warhurst, The Times WN6500 and WN6501

ARMAGEDDON

The Rhine crossing – Operation *Varsity-Plunder* – took place on 23rd March 1945. Second Army assaulted the eastern bank of the river supported by a huge artillery barrage and the dominance of Allied air power. The British 6th and American 17th Airborne Divisions dropped into a stiff fight against fanatical resistance. Once again Churchill came out, this time to gaze on the last great natural barrier on the way to victory. It was a moment of immense personal pride for him to see British troops pouring into the heart of the Reich.

As the Allies approached Münster, *The Times* and *Daily Sketch* photographers were in the same streets picturing American airborne troops riding on British tanks to assault the city. It fell on 3rd April. As the British advance ground on, German towns and villages faced an advancing army in no mood to take unnecessary casualties so near to the end. The fighting was, nonetheless, often confused and bitter and British losses were heavy. By this time some formations had already been broken up to provide reinforcements for others. The pool of British manpower was all but spent and there were no significant reinforcements available. Elsewhere the Canadians with British units attached cleared 'the island' at last and moved up on the Neder Rijn.

By the 17th Arnhem had fallen after a battle launched under the codename Operation *Anger*. The ruined city was taken by men of the British 49th (West Riding) Division – the *Polar Bears*, as ever supported by elements of the specialised 79th Armoured Division using their so-called 'funnies' including Crocodile flamethrower tanks. The Canadians advanced on Apeldoorn and the city fell on the 17th, the day after the liberation of Groningen.

On 15th April forward elements of the British 11th Armoured Division arrived at a scene of horror, the concentration camp at Bergen-Belsen. There they found 13,000 unburied corpses amid over 60,000 people, many of whom were barely alive. Over half of them would die in the following weeks due to starvation and a typhus epidemic that their German and Hungarian guards had done nothing to prevent. Bill Tetlow photographed the nightmare of Belsen but Bill Warhurst did not go there.

The day after reaching Belsen, a much happier ending came with the liberation of prisoner of war camps at Fallingbostel. Stalag XI-B and Stalag 357 housed prisoners from many nationalities with the inmates held in two huge camps. Russian and Italian prisoners had come in for particularly bad treatment at the hands of their guards and many had died. The influx of British and American prisoners after Arnhem and the Battle of the Bulge had swelled numbers to over 100,000. The British Airborne men enforced strict discipline on the other inmates and did their best to improve conditions although food was scarce and sickness was rife. Several thousand men were marched away by the Germans who intended to use them as hostages. The arrival of British armour came none too soon.

The Guards arrived at the huge Marlag und Milag Nord prison camp on 27th April freeing thousands of naval and merchant seamen prisoners. Bill Warhurst filmed the surrender of the commandant and his assistants and the subsequent pleasure of the released prisoners. Numbers had been swelled by over 3,000 men from Stalag-Luft III at Sagan who had been force-marched in advance of the invading Russians. During the final weeks of the advance the Allies were in a race to acquire German military and industrial secrets. Special units were set up for the task and Warhurst encountered the Royal Navy's 30 Assault Unit at Buxtehude, the German navy's administrative headquarters.

To the immense disappointment of his generals Eisenhower had agreed to halt his armies on the Elbe allowing the Russians the glory of taking Berlin. Some on Ike's staff at SHAEF feared the Allies would face large pockets of resistance from clandestine so-called '*Werwolf*' fanatics encouraged by the delusions of Goebbels and other desperate Nazi leaders, but it was not to be. The myth of an Alpine Redoubt never became reality.

By now the end was in sight. On 30th April Adolf Hitler committed suicide as the Red Army closed in and Karl Dönitz, announced his succession as leader after the Führer had 'fallen at his command post'. The Grand Admiral set his regime up at the naval academy in Flensburg to run the remnants of the country in German control from there. Hitler's death was reported in *The Times* on 2nd May alongside a large map showing the remorseless advance of the Allied and Soviet armies. German radio continued to describe the destruction of the Third Reich in Wagnerian tones and compared the defence of Berlin with the Battle of Britain. In Parliament Churchill used classic understatement to describe the war situation in Europe as 'Definitely more satisfactory than it was this time five years ago.'

Photography from this period shows a shattered Germany with a dazed populace coming to terms with total defeat. Warhurst, Clough and Tetlow recorded the chaos of smashed towns and villages as the British crossed the Elbe and headed towards their meeting with the Red Army near Lübeck.

The British pressed on to take Bremerhaven, Bremen and Hamburg. Although the Americans and Russians had linked up at Torgau at the end of April, for Second Army the happy date would be 2nd May when 6th Airborne met the advancing Russians at Wismar. After a tense stand off the smiles broke out

and celebrations could begin. British troops raced into Denmark to secure the country and the cruiser HMS *Birmingham* sailed into Copenhagen to an ecstatic welcome. At Lüneburg Heath Field Marshal Montgomery enjoyed the glory of accepting the surrender of remaining Nazi forces in northern Germany, the Netherlands and Norway. It was his crowning moment.

There followed the surrender of all German forces which took place at Reims in the early hours of 7th May after stalling tactics by the German delegation were rebuffed by an angry General Eisenhower. With the ink dried a cable was sent to the Chiefs of Staffs in London and Washington – a simple understated message to confirm victory in the west.

> *The mission of this Allied Force was fulfilled at 0241,*
> *local time, May 7th, 1945.*
> *EISENHOWER.*

8th May was declared Victory in Europe Day. There were wild scenes in London although the distant war against Japan had four months to run. But on that great day Churchill would stand looking out on Whitehall and tell the huge crowd 'This is your victory!' Many people called back 'No, it is yours.' The scenes in London were photographed by a clutch of photographers from both *The Times* and Kemsley Newspapers. One of them was Eric Greenwood, who had been there at the start in Normandy eleven months earlier. Meanwhile another naval task force was heading to liberate the Channel Islands and with it was Herbert Muggeridge of Kemsley. He recorded the joyous scenes in Guernsey as British troops of Force 135 arrived.

It was over.

TOP The Rhine crossing would see the Allies last great combined land and airborne assault of the war. On the night of 23rd March 1945 British artillery began pounding German positions on the east bank of the river heralding the start of Operation *Plunder*. Bill Warhurst managed to catch the moment a battery of BL5.5inch guns fired together, successfully catching the flashes from three of the guns in his photograph; not bad when we consider he only made two attempts at it.

Herbert W. Warhurst, The Times WN6554

BOTTOM Early next morning and Sherman DD tanks negotiate their way down to the water's edge. Both the Staffordshire Yeomanry and 44th Royal Tank Regiment used them on *Plunder*.

Herbert W. Warhurst, The Times WN6571

TOP Men of 2nd Battalion Seaforth Highlanders, 51st (Highland) Division cross the river.

Herbert W. Warhurst, The Times WN6569

BOTTOM The Allied XVIII Airborne Corps carried out Operation *Varsity* in conjunction with *Plunder*. Two airborne divisions, the US 17th and the British 6th, were deployed and achieved their objectives in the face of stiff resistance. This image shows Waco gliders of the 17th Airborne Division approaching their landing zones.

R. H. Clough, Kemsley E6558

Specially trained Liberator bomber crews of the US 8th Air Force carried out low-level resupply missions in support of operations on the east bank of the Rhine. William Field visited RAF Shipdham in Norfolk to photograph the men and machines of 66th Bombardment Squadron. *L–R*: Lieutenant E. J. White, Lieutenant J. G. Murray and Lieutenant J. Bedes. Murray said 'Everything on the east side of the Rhine seemed to have gone up in smoke and flames.' Bedes reported he had flown low enough – around 400 feet – to see German prisoners marched off with their hands above their heads.

William Field, Kemsley M4261G

LEFT This image looks almost like a page from a catalogue for 79th Armoured Division. The modified Sherman BARV in the foreground has lost its upper works. To the right, a pair of gutted carriers illustrate the pragmatism of Percy Hobart's men. A number of obsolete reconnaissance-role carriers were completely stripped for use as fully tracked trailers for Churchill AVREs.

Herbert W. Warhurst, The Times WN6595

RIGHT   Bill Warhurst takes a break to enjoy a quick smoke on the banks of the Rhine. It is safe to assume the Bren gun is not his!
The Times WN6600

Much to his intense disappointment Winston Churchill was rebuffed when he lobbied senior commanders to be present on D-Day. His visits to the Normandy beachhead were a headache for Montgomery who had much more important things to do than babysit a dewy-eyed PM eager to be part of historic days. Churchill had peed on the Siegfried Line but the Rhine crossing gave him an opportunity to underline his personal crusade against Hitler and nobody could persuade him to keep away. Churchill clearly loved his adventure crossing the Rhine by LVT Buffalo and his banter with appreciative troops gave Bill Warhurst some great moments to record.

Herbert W. Warhurst, The Times WN6604 and WN6607

The Rhine crossing was a challenge met, like so many others, with alacrity by the men of the Royal Engineers. The Allies had in their arsenal one of the most important examples of British engineering to come out of the war – the Bailey bridge. Although Donald Bailey's concept was subject to dispute over patents and elements of the design, the basis of it gave the Allies an edge in the face of bridges demolished by retreating Germans. The Bailey bridge could be assembled without specialised tools or the need for cranes and lends itself to the image of a life-size Meccano set. Sappers are seen fitting the decking to a Class 40 bridge.

R. H. Clough, Kemsley M4261J

Lorries cross the bridge.

R. H. Clough, Kemsley E6555

LEFT A column of Kangaroos carrying men of the 9th Battalion Durham Light Infantry pass a quad 20mm Flakvierling 38 left behind by retreating Germans at Gemund.

Herbert W. Warhurst, The Times WN6619

TOP RIGHT Just a year on from the image of B-17s we saw at the beginning of the book the 'twilight of the Luftwaffe' was confirmed when these abandoned Messerschmitts were found at Wuppertal.

Kemsley E6592

BOTTOM RIGHT Bill Tetlow did not record where this image of infantry passing a Sherman Firefly was taken. They appear to be Canadian and it is likely the Firefly, complete with Duckbill track extensions, is from the British Columbia Regiment.

H. William Tetlow, Kemsley E6586

LEFT By the beginning of April, the British Second Army, supported by the two airborne divisions deployed during *Varsity*, were close to the outskirts of Münster. The city would be assaulted by the US 17th Airborne Division supported by 6th Guards Tank Brigade. Bill Warhurst and Bill Tetlow were present when units formed up for the assault in the recently captured village of Appelhülsen. The two men worked in the same streets as the battle progressed and on 2nd April they photographed men of 513rd Parachute Infantry Regiment climbing on Churchill tanks and M10 Achilles tank destroyers of 4th Tank Battalion Coldstream Guards ready for the advance. Armed with a 17-pounder gun, the Achilles supplemented the less powerfully armed Churchills that were generally incapable of knocking out Panthers and Tigers. Bill Warhurst stood on the deck of an Achilles to take this image of paratroopers making themselves comfortable on a Churchill.

Herbert Warhurst, The Times WN6648

RIGHT Incredibly, Bill Tetlow took this classic shot of the same Churchill seen on the left in the previous picture. The realisation that these two images matched was the genesis of the author's wish to write this book.

H. William Tetlow, Kemsley M4261J

LEFT Germans go into captivity on the outskirts of Münster.

H. William Tetlow, Kemsley E7701

TOP RIGHT As the tanks and paratroopers advanced into the burning city Bill Tetlow caught the moment a Panzerfaust round narrowly missed a Churchill.

H. William Tetlow, Kemsley M4261J (print)

BOTTOM RIGHT Münster burns. Bill Warhurst was further down the street taking a similar scene as Bill Tetlow captured this company of paratroopers passing by.

H. William Tetlow, Kemsley M4261J (print)

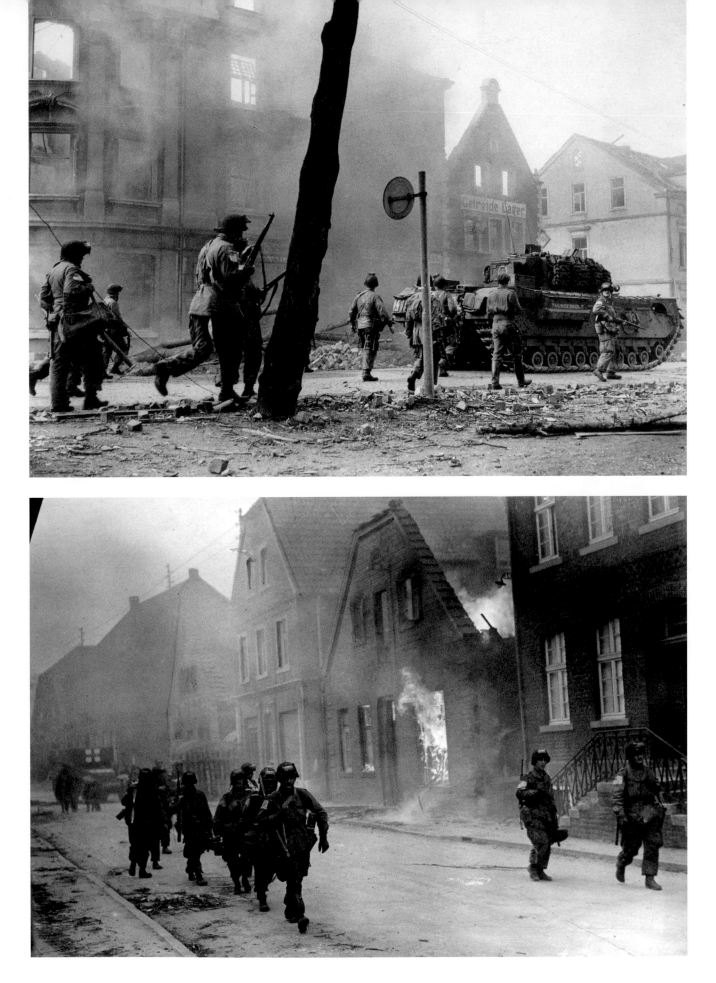

LEFT Captured German officers are searched and questioned. One of them appears willing to provide information.
H. William Tetlow, Kemsley E7711 and E7706

RIGHT More prisoners. One has placed a safe conduct pass dropped by Allied aircraft on the peak of his cap.
H. William Tetlow, Kemsley E7710

TOP Civilians flee the city. The expressions of the children tell their own story.

H. William Tetlow, Kemsley M4261J (print)

BOTTOM The face of defeat: An image like this would be tightly cropped for publication and in fact the darkroom print is a close-in upright image. The full frame is much more pleasing but it is of a style the *Daily Sketch* were unlikely to run without cropping.

H. William Tetlow, Kemsley E7713

One man happy to see the fall of Münster was Trooper Frank Morton of 3rd Reconnaissance Regiment. American paratroopers released him from the barracks where he had been held for a few days since he had been captured. He kept hold of the flag from the building as a souvenir.

H. William Tetlow, Kemsley M4261J

THE LIBERATION OF EUROPE 1944–1945

TOP LEFT Five years in captivity had ended for these happy Belgian soldiers.
Herbert W. Warhurst, The Times WN6653

BOTTOM LEFT These Londoners of 1st Battalion Rifle Brigade were all smiles posing with a bust of Hitler on their M5 half-track.
Herbert W. Warhurst, The Times WN6664

RIGHT After Münster, 6th Guards Tank Brigade had a brief halt for maintenance and replenishment. This, one of three images from the moment, has been posed up for a typical *Daily Sketch* shot. The willing participants are from 4th Tank Battalion Grenadier Guards.
H. William Tetlow, Kemsley E7569

TOP LEFT Units of British XII Corps took Osnabrück on 4th April. Marines of 45 (RM) Commando rustle up a snack on a siding at the railway station. Most of them have acquired German pistols. The city remained a British garrison until 2008.

Herbert W. Warhurst, The Times WN6677

BOTTOM LEFT The advance by XII Corps was checked at Rethem on 10th and 11th April when the sailors and marines of 2.Marine-Infanterie-Division bloodied the nose of 158th Infantry Brigade. The division was made up largely of naval personnel combed from depots and redundant warships but despite little combat experience they handled themselves with typical German accomplishment. There was bitter hand-to-hand fighting for Rethem with both sides suffering heavy casualties. British troops were instructed to carry out a succession of assaults that cost them dear. 1st/5th Battalion Welch Regiment suffered particularly badly and the situation was made worse by allegations of war crimes against the Germans for the supposed murder of British prisoners. *The Times* ran a story on 11th April giving an eye-witness account of the murders by Private James Parry from Newport who claimed to have seen the men being machine-gunned with their own weapons by 'SS troops'. The blame was placed on men of an SS training battalion, a highly motivated group of junior leaders who had fought with customary determination since the Rhine crossing. As it turned out what Private Parry had taken to be the killing of prisoners was actually German marines putting animals trapped in burning farm buildings out of their misery. The captured British soldiers were treated with care and the misunderstanding was cleared up when an officer managed to escape to British lines. This image shows Private James Parry when he gave his account of the 'murders'.

Herbert W. Warhurst, The Times WN6709

RIGHT These exhausted men of 2.Marine-Infanterie-Division were photographed by Bill Warhurst on 11th April 1945.

Herbert Warhurst, The Times WN6713

LEFT Hundreds of miles away from Germany, pockets of resistance continued to hold out on the French Atlantic coast. We saw cordial events during the siege of St Nazaire back in January but at Royan, on the mouth of the Gironde, attempts to take the city would lead to its virtual destruction. In January much of the city had been devastated by an attack by 350 RAF bombers ordered in by SHAEF. During the final assault beginning on 14th April American heavy bombers attacked on consecutive days using high explosives and then napalm with predictable results for both the defenders and unfortunate civilians trapped in the city. It was the only occasion the US 8th Air Force used the new weapon during the war. The reduction of the Royan Pocket was entrusted to General Philippe Leclerc's veteran 2e Division Blindée who had liberated Paris in August 1944. Leclerc's polyglot force of French, North Africans and exiled Spanish Republicans fought their way into the ruined city accompanied by Frederick Skinner. The French armour goes in with infantry clinging on the back.

Frederick R. Skinner, Kemsley E7726

TOP RIGHT Troops moving on roads choked with dust.

Frederick R. Skinner, Kemsley E7727

BOTTOM RIGHT French troops pick their way through the ruins of Royan.

Frederick R. Skinner, Kemsley print

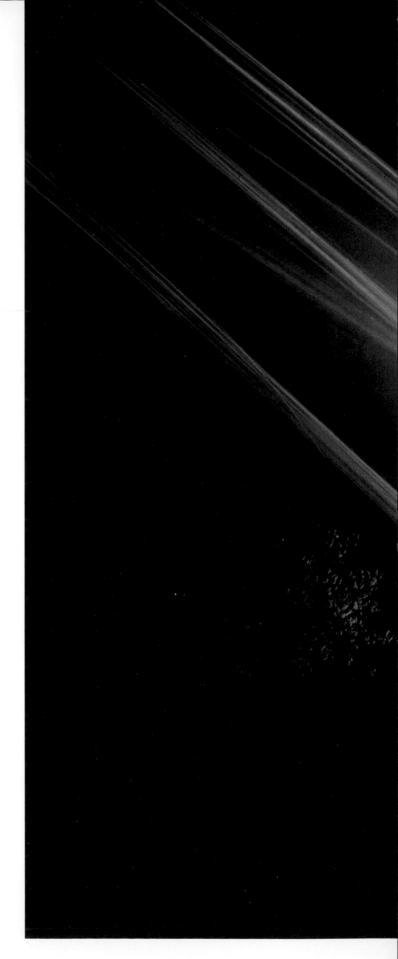

In the Netherlands the battle to clear 'the island' and liberate the ruins of Arnhem was under way on 12th April. The attack, codenamed Operation *Anger*, was launched by 49th (West Riding) Infantry Division. It opened with a massive artillery barrage covering 56th Infantry Brigade crossing the Ijssel witnessed by Bill Tetlow. This picture shows a battery of RP-3 rockets launched from an orchard. These 60lb (27kg) rockets were the same as those carried by Allied aircraft in the ground-attack role and had proved devastating to armoured and soft-skin vehicles.

H. William Tetlow, Kemsley M4261J

TOP LEFT 146th Infantry Brigade men prepare for their part in the assault on Arnhem. The carriers are from 4th Battalion Lincolnshire Regiment and include two Wasp MkIIC flamethrowers.

H. William Tetlow, Kemsley M4261J

BOTTOM LEFT 17th April 1945. The 'Funnies' of 79th Armoured Division supported the assault on Arnhem. Here a newsreel cameraman films a Humber Scout Car of 1st Lothians & Border Horse passing through burning ruins.

H. William Tetlow, Kemsley E6571

TOP RIGHT A soldier looks at the remains of the Arnhem Bridge, the 'bridge too far', scene of heroics by men of 2nd Battalion Parachute Regiment and other elements of British 1st Airborne Division during *Market Garden*. American bombers destroyed the bridge on 7th October 1944 to deny it to the enemy.

H. William Tetlow, Kemsley E6575

BOTTOM RIGHT Another of Bill Tetlow's classic images shows the grave of an unknown airborne soldier encountered after the liberation of Arnhem.

H. William Tetlow, Kemsley E6574

LEFT The name of Belsen is synonymous with the barbarity of the Nazi regime. During the advance into Germany, the Chief Medical Officer of Second Army, Brigadier Glyn Hughes, had vague ideas that the concentration camp at Bergen-Belsen would present challenges but nothing could prepare him for the scenes of horror found when British troops entered the camp on 15th April 1945. Hughes later said 'No photograph, no description, could bring home the horrors I saw.' It is convenient to assume that the scale of the death and suffering may have defeated Bill Tetlow because he appears to have taken very few images at Belsen. Another witness was the BBC's Richard Dimbleby, whose chilling report from the camp remains harrowing listening. He described it as the most horrible day of his life. Although Belsen was not a death camp like Auschwitz, the Germans did nothing to prevent the spread of typhus and other infectious diseases among the overcrowded and starving inmates. There were 60,000 crammed into the camp when the British arrived and the bodies of 13,000 others had been left out in the open. Five hundred more died each day following the liberation despite the best efforts of Hughes and his staff.

H. William Tetlow, Kemsley E6603

RIGHT Tetlow recorded the first religious service held at the camp after liberation.

H. William Tetlow, Kemsley E6604

LEFT On 16th April the tanks of 8th King's Royal Irish Hussars arrived at another huge camp, the vast Stalags XI-B and 357 at Fallingbostel where over 90,000 prisoners of war had been housed before the Germans marched thousands away from the Allied advance to use them as a bargaining chips. The camps held prisoners from a rainbow of nationalities with men captured during *Market Garden*, the Battle of the Bulge and other actions adding to the numbers. Despite the onset of malnutrition and disease the prisoners were naturally ecstatic to be freed and the opportunities for positive images were plentiful.

Herbert W. Warhurst, The Times WN6743

TOP RIGHT British Airborne prisoners captured at Arnhem had been busy imposing their brand of discipline on the camp since arriving and their esprit de corps never dimmed. This group were especially pleased to meet Sergeant Denis Smith of the Army Film & Photographic Unit. He had been fortunate to escape the besieged perimeter at Oosterbeek during the sad end of *Market Garden*, bringing back with him a number of classic photographs that have become standard images appearing in many Second World War histories.

Herbert W. Warhurst, The Times WN6730

BOTTOM RIGHT The regime at Fallingbostel treated Soviet prisoners with a mixture of indifference and harshness and many died as a result of neglect or brutality. Italians, too, came in for rough treatment. After liberation one of the first tasks was to give the victims a decent burial.

H. William Tetlow, Kemsley E7561

TOP LEFT The town of Fallingbostel came under attack by 7th Armoured Division. A Challenger tank of 8th King's Royal Irish Hussars is seen outside the town while the crew have a quick brew, 18th April 1945. Although derived from the Cromwell, the large turret needed to house a QF 17-pounder gun necessitated a longer hull with an additional road wheel to take the weight. Only 200 of the Tank, Cruiser Mk VIII, Challenger were built. Despite being reliable and popular with crews the proliferation of the equivalent but cheaper Sherman Vc Firefly made it uneconomical to produce more.

Herbert W. Warhurst. The Times WN6746

BOTTOM LEFT A 16-year-old serving with the SS is taken prisoner at Fallingbostel.

Herbert W. Warhurst, The Times WN6749

RIGHT A feature of the last month of the war was the race for German military and industrial secrets carried out by the Anglo-Americans and the Soviet Union. It was a serious business for the British with specialist units from T-Force branching out across the Reich to secure scientists, technicians and anyone of interest in addition to documents and hardware. Bill Warhurst happened to catch the Royal Navy's secretive 30 Assault Unit when he arrived at the Kriegsmarine's administrative headquarters at Buxtehude on 22nd April. He photographed Konteradmiral Siegfried Engel, the Deputy Commanding Admiral North Sea, being taken into custody by Lieutenant Commander Dunstan Curtis who seems a little unpleased to have been snapped. Curtis was a swashbuckling character with a reputation for action, earning him a DSC at St Nazaire in 1942. He was a friend of Ian Fleming and there is some suggestion he is one of the influences for James Bond.

Herbert W. Warhurst, The Times WN6773

TOP An aircraft as stripped and heavily damaged as this Messerschmitt Me262 could still yield valuable components.
Herbert W. Warhurst, The Times WN6768

BOTTOM There were other things of interest. This relatively undamaged V2 rocket was a valuable find.
R. H. Clough, Kemsley M4261J

TOP The fall of Bremen on 26th April offered much more. These prefabricated U-Boat sections were photographed by Bill Tetlow.

H. William Tetlow, Kemsley M4264A

BOTTOM The British had some intriguing weapons of their own. The 1st Tank Battalion Coldstream Guards modified some of their Shermans to accommodate rails for two RP-3 rockets on the turret. These tanks were given the name Tulip. The rockets were fairly inaccurate when fired in this manner but the effect must have had its merits.

H. William Tetlow, Kemsley M4264A

A much-favoured and evocative way to illustrate the collapse of the Reich is found in images showing Allied armour passing German prisoners on the autobahn. The 8th King's Royal Irish Hussars obliged the camera of Bill Tetlow on the road near Hollenstedt en route to Hamburg.

H. William Tetlow, Kemsley M4261J

LEFT The Marlag-Milag prisoner-of-war camp complex at Westertimke was liberated by units of the Guards Armoured Divison on 27th April. Marlag und Milag was a twin camp for naval prisoners and merchant mariner internees, the majority of them British. In this image the blindfolded camp commandant Kapitan-zur-See W. Rugge and his chief of staff Zahlmeister Leutnant H. Heuken are brought in to negotiate the surrender of the camp with British officers.

Herbert W. Warhurst, The Times WN6789

TOP RIGHT Two happy men liberated that day were recipients of the Victoria Cross awarded for their actions commanding midget submarines during the attack on the battleship *Tirpitz* on 22nd September 1943. Lieutenant Godfrey Place RN commanding X7 *Pdinichthys* and Lieutenant Donald Cameron RNR commanding X6 *Piker II* entered Kåfjord in north Norway negotiating a minefield and evading anti-submarine nets before placing their charges. The *Tirpitz* was severely damaged as a result of their actions although other midget submarines on the operation did not reach the target.

Herbert W. Warhurst, The Times WN6798

BOTTOM RIGHT This image shows Lieutenant Michael Wynn, DSC, the future 7th Baron Newborough, with Chief Motor Mechanic Bill Lovegrove. They were captured during the St Nazaire raid of 1942 where Wynn's life had been saved by Lovegrove. Wynn, who lost an eye on the raid, had been held in Colditz after escaping from Marlag Nord. He was repatriated after feigning illness and returned with Second Army when the liberation of Marlag Nord was imminent to find the man who had saved his life in 1942. Bill Lovegrove was awarded the Conspicuous Gallantry Medal for his action during the raid. 'Micky' Wynn lived a colourful life after the war. His ashes were fired from a cannon in Istanbul following his death in 1998.

Herbert W. Warhurst, The Times WN6800

LEFT The British crossed the Elbe on 29th April. One of the vehicles being ferried across is a captured Sd.Kfz.251. These versatile half-tracks were much appreciated by the Allies and often put to good use. The image has been censored with sticky paper applied over the skyline.

R. H. Clough, Kemsley M4267X

RIGHT The men of the Recce Troop, 3rd Tank Battalion, Scots Guards, 6th Guards Tank Brigade pose with their Stuart tanks amid the ruins of a German town.

Kemsley M4264A

TOP LEFT The demarcation line for British and Soviet forces ended at Lübeck on the Baltic but there was concern that Marshal Konstantin Rokossovsky's 2nd Belorussian Front would push on into Denmark. British units reached Lübeck on 2nd May 1945 and advanced to Wismar where leading elements of 6th Airborne Division met the Russians. After the first tense encounters there were smiles all round. The war was not over, but the victory at all costs Winston Churchill demanded when he spoke in Parliament on 13th May 1940 had come to pass. Here a group of military policemen of 6th Airborne greet Soviet troops riding on an ISU122 self-propelled gun.

Herbert W. Warhurst, The Times WN6992

BOTTOM LEFT There was fun to be had cleaning the barrel of a T34/85.

Herbert W. Warhurst, The Times WN6991

RIGHT All smiles: a Russian female soldier poses with 6th Airborne men including some from the 1st (Airborne) Battalion Ulster Rifles, the Corps of Military Police, a signaller and two Canadian gunners. The man linking arms with the Russian lady is Captain Frank Garstang, a forward observer with the Royal Artillery.

Herbert Warhurst, The Times WN6976

A number of French prisoners of war were released at Mölln on 3rd May and they immediately began accusing their former guards of ill treatment. While the guards were being lined up the wife of one them fell to her knees and begged British soldiers for his life, under the impression her husband was about to be shot. This appears to have been much to the amusement of a former prisoner.

H. William Tetlow, Kemsley E6680

LEFT With Hitler dead Grossadmiral Karl Dönitz became German head of state. He set up his government at the Mürwick Naval Academy at Flensburg on 2nd May and sent Generaladmiral Hans-Georg von Friedeburg to negotiate terms of the surrender of German forces with Montgomery at Lüneburg Heath. But Monty made it clear that the only option available to the Germans was unconditional surrender. Dönitz signalled his agreement and von Friedeburg signed the instrument of surrender of all German forces in the Netherlands, north-west Germany and Denmark on 4th May 1945. The admiral and his delegation arrive at Lüneburg.

H. William Tetlow, Kemsley M4264A

TOP RIGHT Monty explains the details as the Germans look on.

Herbert W. Warhurst, The Times WN6935

BOTTOM RIGHT Surrender: Montgomery and von Friedeburg watch General Eberhard Kinzel signing the instrument on behalf of the German army. Monty's interpreter Joe Ewart stands on the left.

H. William Tetlow, Daily Sketch M4264A

TOP LEFT News of the surrender quickly spreads.

Kemsley print

BOTTOM LEFT The news from Lüneburg Heath had an immediate impact in Denmark where patriots were pictured rounding up a group of SS men who had changed into civilian clothing.

H. William Tetlow, Kemsley E7555

RIGHT Ecstatic crowds in Denmark greet the end of German occupation.
H. William Tetlow, Kemsley M4264E

THE LIBERATION OF EUROPE 1944–1945

LEFT Although he had approved the surrender of German forces at Lüneburg, Karl Dönitz resisted any similar arrangements with the Russians. It suited him to play for time and in doing so attempt to drive a wedge between East and West. But on 6th May Eisenhower insisted there would be no similar agreements giving the Soviets grounds to believe the Anglo-Americans were seeking a separate peace. He demanded the Germans send a delegation to his headquarters at Reims for surrender talks where he called for the immediate and simultaneous surrender of all German forces. Senior negotiator General Alfred Jodl demurred but an impatient Eisenhower warned him that if the Germans did not accept his terms, his armies would go back on the offensive and, portentously, he would close Allied lines to Germans retreating westward. Jodl informed Dönitz the game was up and, accordingly, the instrument of surrender was signed at 0241hrs on 7th May 1945. But the Russians were unhappy with the terms agreed at Reims. They demanded the Germans be made to surrender formally in Berlin, the city where their disastrous war of aggression had been planned. Eisenhower agreed and so the German signatories were flown to Berlin to do it all again on 8th May. In London Churchill broadcasted to the nation on 7th May to announce the surrender and declare the 8th as Victory in Europe Day. Pockets of German resistance continued in French ports and elsewhere and there were myriad ends to tie up. Frederick Skinner was at Reims to witness the moment when Alfred Jodl signed for the Germans and Lieutenant-General Walter Bedell Smith, Ike's Chief of Staff, signed on his behalf. Jodl is flanked by Generaladmiral von Friedeburg and Major Wilhelm Oxenius, the operations officer for Panzergruppe West.

Frederick R. Skinner, Kemsley M4264A

RIGHT The victors.

R. H. Clough, Kemsley E6583

News of victory brought crowds out onto the
Champs-Élysées.

Frederick R. Skinner, Kemsley E6560

THE LIBERATION OF EUROPE 1944–1945

TOP LEFT The king and the architects of victory: There was a mixture of pride and relief in London on VE Day where HM King George VI lined up with Churchill and the armed forces chiefs. But the fight against Japan had months to run and much of Europe was in ruins. There was an awful lot yet to do. The three chiefs are Marshal of the Royal Air Force Sir Charles Portal, Field Marshal Sir Alan Brooke and Admiral of the Fleet Sir Andrew Cunningham.

J. Kirby, Kemsley M4264H

BOTTOM LEFT Victory left a very important loose end to tie up. The liberation of the Channel Islands went by the somewhat whimsical name of Operation *Nestegg*. The veteran destroyer HMS *Bulldog,* with Herbert Muggeridge aboard, arrived off St Peter Port, Guernsey on 8th May carrying lead elements of Force 135 under command of Brigadier Alfred Snow. The commander of the Channel Islands, Vizeadmiral Friedrich Hüffmeier, refused to take orders from the British but sent an emissary, Kapitanleutnant Armin Zimmerman, to discuss terms. Just after midnight the second in command of the islands, Generalmajor Siegfried Heine came aboard and agreed to surrender and Snow's men went ashore at 0845hrs. This image shows an early stage in negotiations with Zimmerman facing Brigadier Snow and his staff.

Herbert Muggeridge, Kemsley M4246Q

RIGHT Crowds cheer British troops in St Peter Port.

Herbert Muggeridge, Kemsley M4264Q

TOP There was joy for Guernsey man Petty Officer J. D. Langlois when his sister Alice greeted him for the first time in five years.

Herbert Muggeridge, Kemsley M4264Q

BOTTOM A much less happier man was Vizeadmiral Hüffmeier, seen being escorted from his headquarters. He showed his contempt for the surrender and his captors by destroying his sword. He had, at one time, been a less than successful captain of the battleship *Scharnhorst* where he was deeply unpopular.

Herbert Muggeridge, Kemsley M4264Q

VICTORY

Men and women of the Allied Expeditionary Forces:

The crusade on which we embarked in the early summer of 1944 has reached its glorious conclusion. It is my special privilege, in the name of all Nations represented in this Theater of War, to commend each of you for valiant performance of duty. Though these words are feeble they come from the bottom of a heart overflowing with pride in your loyal service and admiration for you as warriors.... Let us have no part in the profitless quarrels in which other men inevitably engage as to what country, what service, won the European War. Every man, every woman, of every nation here represented, has served according to his or her ability, and the efforts of each have contributed to the outcome. This we shall remember – and in doing so we shall be revering each honored grave, and be sending comfort to the loved ones of comrades who could not live to see this day. General Dwight D Eisenhower. Victory Order of the Day. 08. 05. 1945.

With the celebrations over the Allies had to get on with running the defeated Germany. Thousands of former prisoners of war and displaced persons were desperate to return home. Disarming German forces would take time. The thorny issue of what to do with the German leadership was resolved by direct action. On 22nd May units of the British 11th Armoured Division rounded up the Flensburg government using tanks to make an impression upon anyone silly enough to pick a fight with them. The key figures, Karl Dönitz, Alfred Jodl and Albert Speer were paraded for the press in a humiliating end to the thousand-year Reich they had served so loyally. Having signed the surrenders at Lüneburg, Reims and Berlin this latest humiliation was all too much for Admiral Hans Georg von Friedeberg and he committed suicide. Alfred Jodl was hanged after Nuremberg.

Down the road at Lüneburg a group of former Russian POWs handed over a man they had picked up at a roadblock to the British authorities. The Russians were very suspicious about his identity and they were right to be, for the man wearing a Luftwaffe sergeant's uniform was none other than Heinrich Himmler. After a short time in British custody the former Reichsführer admitted his true identity. A doctor was called to examine him and as this took place Himmler bit on a cyanide capsule he had hidden from his captors. Bill Warhurst was on hand to photograph the corpse.

Elsewhere the propagandist William Joyce, the much-reviled 'Lord Haw-Haw' was captured and brought to Lüneburg where he was treated for a gunshot wound to the buttocks. He was photographed a while later looking reasonably relaxed but he could expect no mercy and was hanged for treason at Wandsworth Prison in 1946. On the day of Himmler's death a U-boat sailed up the River Thames for public inspection at Westminster Pier. Many more came in to surrender at British ports and the vast majority were eventually scuttled off the Irish coast. The next day British newspapers reported an imminent cut in the meat ration. Food rationing would remain a feature of British life until 1954.

Bill Warhurst's final act in Germany was to film the disbandment of the Guards Armoured Division in June. The division paraded with its armoured vehicles for Monty and then gave them up as the Guards reverted to their traditional roles. Montgomery stayed on for a year as the first commander of the British Army of the Rhine, a force that was not disbanded until May 1994.

July saw the start of the Potsdam Conference when the victorious Allies gathered to agree on the future of Europe. The event signalled an end of days for Winston Churchill as he lost the 'victory election' to Clement Attlee. The two-week conference represented a lot of work for Bill Tetlow but he succeeded in taking some excellent images. He would remain in Germany to photograph the foundation of Allied zones of authority in Berlin.

The campaign in North-West Europe was a huge undertaking involving millions of Allied personnel. Photographers from *The Times* and Kemsley Newspapers had done an amazing job showing many aspects of the campaign but once it was over they did much the same as millions of conscripts and went back to their normal lives. R. H. Clough and Frederick Skinner returned to their stomping grounds in north of England while Bill Tetlow left Kemsley in 1947. Eric Greenwood and Cathal O'Gorman stayed on at *The Times* for the remainder of their careers, retiring in 1966 and 1968 respectively.

The Second World War caused such a spike in material that by the early 1970s the librarians at Times Newspapers were running out of space so an edit was made of the plate negative collection to create room for expansion. Roy Thomson had acquired *The Sunday Times* in 1959 and *The Times* seven years later. In the case of *The Times*, 'neg diaries' show many deletions, especially from the wartime period. Happily the importance of the campaign in 1944/45 was appreciated and the work of Bill Warhurst, Eric Greenwood and Cathal O'Gorman survives. The Kemsley material for the period was also cut back but much of the print archive was retained. These collections form the basis of this book.

It is a sad fact that the press photographers of the campaign in North-West Europe are not well known. While it is wrong to try to interpret what they thought of their adventures they made the most from a series of massive events. Britain's wartime press photographers were rarely given bylines and they did not garner the notoriety of their heirs in Vietnam and beyond. When we look at the huge variety of subjects and events they photographed over the course of long careers it is clear these photographers were masters of their craft and it is not too late to recognise them for being the remarkable men they undoubtedly were.

The German heavy cruiser *Prinz Eugen* marooned at Copenhagen. The ship had arrived in April unable to proceed due to a lack of fuel. It was handed over to the British on 9th May and sailed for Wilhelmshaven later in the month. The cruiser was allotted as a war prize to the United States and became the USS *Prinz Eugen* for a period of examination but mechanical problems and lack of spares were a persistent problem for her mixed American and German crew. The cruiser was added to the fleet of target ships used in atomic bomb tests at Bikini Atoll in 1946 and having survived two bombs the radioactive *Prinz Eugen* was towed to Kwajalein Atoll and capsized over Enubuj reef on 22nd December 1946. The ship is now a popular site for divers.

H. William Tetlow, Kemsley E7549

TOP LEFT A group of SS troops hand in their weapons. The men appear to be from a non-German police unit and seem too cheerful to be Danish volunteers. They are handing in a hotchpotch of weaponry; much of it captured stock, including British Sten guns and American M1 Carbine rifles. The man keeping a watch on events is armed with a Russian SVT-40.

H. William Tetlow, Kemsley (print)

BOTTOM LEFT Danes make it clear to departing Germans who their hero is.

H. William Tetlow, Kemsley (print)

RIGHT The man himself lapped up the attention during his visit to Copenhagen when he was feted with a parade through the city.
H. William Tetlow, Kemsley E7393

LEFT The immediate task for the British was to sort out the many thousands of prisoners of war in their area. The last days of the conflict had been known as the 'Great Surrender' as whole divisions walked into captivity joining thousands more trapped west of the Elbe. Roads were choked with all manner of transport in addition to vast columns of people on foot. Both Warhurst and Tetlow took a number of images around the Lüneburg area but neither of them recorded the exact locations. A heavy reliance on the faithful horse by the Germans remained a critical factor in victory and defeat.

Herbert W. Warhurst, The Times WN6916

TOP RIGHT A perch on any motor vehicle was highly prized.

H. William Tetlow, Kemsley E7377

BOTTOM RIGHT By the end of the war German industry was running out of just about everything. With sources of raw materials becoming increasingly scarce the Nazis resorted to recycling any useful metal. R. H. Clough found this pile of church bells in a smelting yard in Hamburg.

R. H. Clough, Kemsley M4267X

Bill Warhurst photographed
these incomplete U-boats at the
Blohm und Voss shipyard.

Herbert W. Warhurst, The Times
WN6964

TOP LEFT The question of what to do with Karl Dönitz's government at Flensburg created tensions within the Alliance. The Russians were uncompromising in their wish to see the leadership arrested but there were some grounds to the argument that retention was temporarily useful for governing the defeated Germany. Major-General Lowell W. Rooks and his team had taken up residence on the liner SS *Patria* to liaise with Dönitz's administration while the debate over its future continued. The argument was settled when General Eisenhower determined that what the Russians called the 'Dönitz Gang' had to go. On 23rd May the leadership were summoned to the *Patria* to hear their fate. Generaloberst Alfred Jodl leaving Mürwick Naval Academy for the *Patria*.

Frederick R. Skinner, Kemsley E7730

TOP MIDDLE Dönitz with Generaloberst Alfred Jodl and Generaladmiral Hans-Georg von Friedeburg in the lounge bar of the *Patria* facing Major-General Lowell W. Rooks of the US Army as he reads out the instructions dissolving the Flensburg government and ordering the arrest of senior military and political officials. Standing extreme right is Brigadier Edward Foord, a senior British intelligence officer with SHAEF, sitting to Rooks' left is Major-General Nikolai Trusov of the Soviet Army. Nearest the camera is Captain Guy Maund of the Royal Navy who became head of the British Frontier Service in Germany.

Frederick R. Skinner, Kemsley M4264A

BOTTOM LEFT Dönitz, Jodl and Dr Albert Speer are paraded for the press. All three would face trial at Nuremberg.

Herbert W. Warhurst, The Times WN6850

BOTTOM MIDDLE At Mürwick British troops supported by tanks began rounding up military personnel and officials serving the Flensburg regime.

Frederick R. Skinner, Kemsley E7738

RIGHT The situation was the final straw for Generaladmiral Hans-Georg von Friedeburg. He had surrendered to Monty at Lüneburg on 4th May where he had suffered a nervous breakdown. This was followed by further indignities at Reims and Berlin where his emotional state declined even further. He took prussic acid in a lavatory at Plön on the day of his arrest. A convinced Nazi, the admiral had been deputy commander of the U-boat fleet and was last commander of the Kriegsmarine. In some accounts, he had decided as early as 1944 to take his own life if Germany lost the war. Frederick Skinner took this macabre picture of the admiral after his body had been laid out under the portrait of his boss Dönitz. The scene was also recorded by Margaret Bourke-White of *Life* magazine.

Frederick R. Skinner, Kemsley E7731

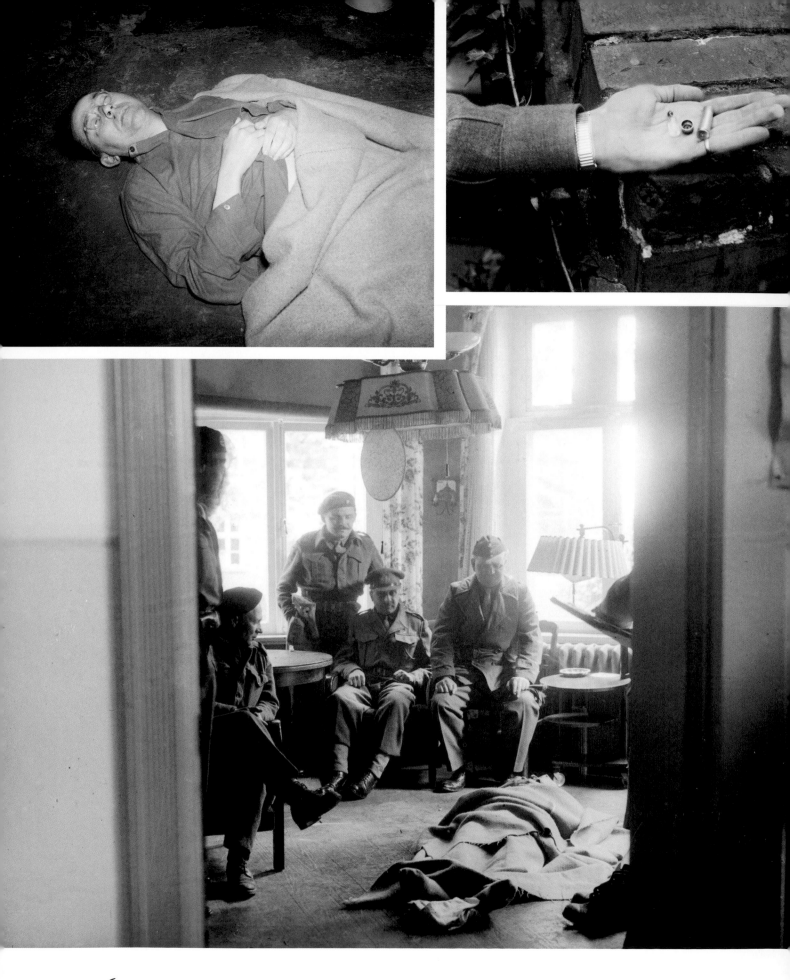

TOP LEFT Former Reichsführer-SS Heinrich Himmler had experienced a rapid fall from grace during the final days of the Third Reich. Hitler had branded him a traitor for seeking to negotiate with the Anglo-Americans, describing it as the 'worst treachery he had ever known.' Himmler believed the western Allies would join Germany against the Russians and held meetings with Count Bernadotte of the Red Cross and Norbert Masur of the World Jewish Congress looking for suitable intermediaries. After Hitler's suicide he attempted to ingratiate himself with Karl Dönitz but the new head of state dismissed him from all his offices the day before the surrender at Reims. On 21st May Himmler and two companions were stopped at a checkpoint manned by former Soviet prisoners of war who were suspicious of the true identity of the man claiming to be a Luftwaffe sergeant named Heinrich Hitzinger. He was delivered to the British at Lüneburg on the 23rd and having admitted his true identity he swallowed a hidden cyanide capsule during a medical examination. He took fifteen minutes to die. Bill Warhurst photographed the corpse.

Herbert W. Warhurst, The Times WN6869

BOTTOM LEFT R. H. Clough took this surreal scene of Allied officers sitting with Himmler's body.

R. H. Clough, Kemsley M4267X

TOP MIDDLE A press conference was called where the container for the cyanide was produced.

Herbert W. Warhurst, The Times WN6873

RIGHT Himmler's companions were two men with a story to tell. On the left is his aide-de-camp, 29-year-old Obersturmbannführer Werner Grothmann. On the right is 24-year-old Sturmbannführer Heinz Macher, a decorated combat veteran chosen as one of Himmler's assistants. One of his last duties was to destroy the Nazi shrine at Wewelsburg Castle.

H. William Tetlow, Kemsley M4267X

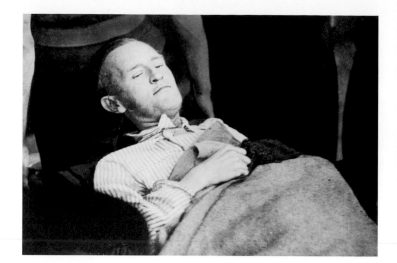

TOP LEFT AND MIDDLE The Nazi propagandist William Joyce, known as 'Lord Haw-Haw', was hiding in woodland near Flensburg when British soldiers challenged him on 28th May. He was shot in the buttocks while reaching for his passport and taken to Lüneburg for medical treatment and held there for interrogation. Joyce's wife Margaret, a propagandist and vehement supporter of the Nazis, gave herself up the next day. Bill Warhurst provided these images of them in custody.

Herbert W. Warhurst, The Times WN6861 and WN6864A

TOP RIGHT Warhurst photographed Joyce out for a stroll under guard some time later. Although born in the USA, Joyce had returned to his father's native Ireland as a child and was a staunch Unionist. Moving to England during the 1920s he embraced the far right and became a leading figure in the British Union of Fascists with a reputation for brawling and aggressive oratory. He was sacked from his position as deputy leader by Oswald Mosley in 1937 and travelled to Germany with his wife before the outbreak of war. Joyce's broadcasts to Britain achieved an audience of millions but he was widely seen as a somewhat sinister figure of fun. He was, nevertheless, held to be a traitor and as such he could have had little hope of evading justice. Joyce was hanged for high treason at Wandsworth Prison in January 1946.

Herbert W. Warhurst, The Times WN6863

BOTTOM LEFT There were other unsavoury characters. Thomas Haller Cooper, also known as Tom Böttcher, was an Anglo-German fascist who served in various SS units on the Eastern Front between 1941 and 1943 when he was seriously wounded. He received the Wound Badge in silver and is the only British person to have been awarded a Nazi combat decoration. He was involved in the creation of the tiny British Free Corps, working with John Amery and others. Disowned by the Nazis he remained serving in the armed forces until the end of the war. Cooper surrendered to the Americans on 2nd May and was handed over to the British. He was tried for high treason in 1946 and sentenced to death but this was commuted to life imprisonment. He was released in 1953.

Herbert W. Warhurst, The Times WN6865

BOTTOM RIGHT Germany could not operate without formal government and so agreement was reached between the United States, Soviet Union, United Kingdom and France to set up the Allied Control Council to run the country through the respective occupation zones of the four powers. Just a year after the launch of Operation *Overlord*, General Eisenhower and Field Marshal Montgomery signed the treaty ratifying the new system of government in Berlin, in the company of Marshal Georgiy Zhukov and General Jean de Lattre de Tassigny on 5th June 1945. The four then posed for photographs.

H. William Tetlow, Kemsley E6598

Bill Warhurst attended the Farewell to Armour parade held on Rotenburg Airfield near Hamburg by the Guards Armoured Division and 6th Guards Tank Brigade on 9th June 1945. The parade marked reversion to their traditional role by the Household infantry battalions that had converted to armour for the campaign in North-West Europe. Field Marshal Montgomery inspected every unit on parade and spoke to the men. This join-up was published in *The Times* on 11th June. Warhurst returned to the UK and, like the Guards, he went back to doing his usual job. He had taken 2,000 images during the campaign.

Herbert W. Warhurst, The Times WN6807

TOP LEFT Sherman Firefly crews from 2nd Tank Battalion Scots Guards.

Herbert W. Warhurst, The Times WN6810

BOTTOM LEFT It seems appropriate at this point to include this image of the Manx ferry *Ben-my-Chree* arriving at Dover with men selected for demobilisation on 18th June 1945. Built in 1927, she was a Dunkirk veteran and had taken part in the D-Day landings embarking the US Army Rangers who carried out the legendary assault on Pointe du Hoc. We saw Canadian assault troops for D-Day boarding her sister ship *Lady of Mann* at the beginning of this book.

Robert Chandler, Kemsley M4267J

RIGHT Home at last. A group of soldiers are very happy to be back on British soil.
Robert Chandler, Kemsley M4267J

TOP Married women serving in the Women's Royal Naval Service on their way to demobilise at the WRNS discharge depot at Hampstead in London on 18th June 1945. *L–R*: Cora McHugh of Devon, Grace Powell of Surrey, Evelyn Humphrey of Sheffield and Joan Nicholas of Lee-on-Solent.

Sidney Beadell, Kemsley M4267I

BOTTOM Great War veteran George Allfree was an anti-aircraft gunner from Walworth in south London who had served in the Territorial Army between the wars and had been called up in 1939. Albert Abrahams' caption tells us George was looking forward to a holiday before returning to his job as a commissionaire. He is pictured trying on a hat to go with his demob suit.

Albert Abrahams, Kemsley M4267I

LEFT There was a long journey home for the Americans before they could return to civilian life. One man adds his name to countless others on the guardrail of the RMS *Queen Elizabeth* in Southampton just before she set sail for New York.

Robert Chandler, Kemsley M4273S

RIGHT A soldier enjoys a farewell kiss on the quayside. Both these images appeared in the *Sunday Graphic* on 26th August 1945, another newspaper in Lord Kemsley's extensive stable.

Robert Chandler, Kemsley M4273S

TOP LEFT Agreeing to jointly govern Germany was one thing, having a plan was a different matter altogether. The victorious nations met at Potsdam to discuss the future of Germany and a good deal else besides. Bill Tetlow was on hand to record some of the background events, following Churchill and Ernest Bevin on what we now term photo calls and there were other attractions. Although it is disappointing to note he did not photograph the 'Big Three' together, Tetlow did some fine work.

H. William Tetlow, Kemsley M4270C

BOTTOM LEFT A Russian guide gives Churchill and his daughter Mary a tour of the ruins of Hitler's Chancellery.

H. William Tetlow, Kemsley M4270C

RIGHT There was grim satisfaction for Churchill when he arrived at the place where the bodies of Hitler and Eva Braun were burnt.
H. William Tetlow, Kemsley M4270C

TOP Colourful stories have persisted for decades that Hitler escaped from Berlin and there were doubts at the time that he had committed suicide. A policeman named Hermann Karnau claimed to have seen the bodies of the Führer and his bride while they were burned. He is pictured being questioned by Sergeant Otto Almasy and Captain Kenneth Leslie. Although he changed details of his story a number of times, Karnau's description is broadly consistent with the known facts of Hitler's death.

H. William Tetlow, Kemsley M4267S

BOTTOM Ernest Bevin pictured in Hitler's study looking at the remains of a large ornate desk.

H. William Tetlow, Kemsley M4271V

TOP ATS 'girls' working in the British compound at Potsdam were given a half-day off to visit the Chancellery. Here Lance Corporal Ruby Matchison and a friend inspect film from Hitler's private cinema.

H. William Tetlow, Kemsley M4270T

BOTTOM Souvenir hunting was the order of the day. Margaret Patrick of Long Sutton in Lincolnshire and Olive Palmer of North Walsham in Norfolk seem pleased with pieces of a chandelier from the Chancellery.

H. William Tetlow, Kemsley M4271T

One of the highlights of Churchill's time in Berlin was the victory parade on 21st July where Major-General Lewis Lyne's 7th Armoured Division – *the Desert Rats* – put on a great show for the prime minister. He returned the compliment telling them 'Dear Desert Rats! May your glory ever shine! May your laurels never fade! May the memory of this glorious pilgrimage of war which you have made from Alamein, via the Baltic to Berlin never die!' The Challenger and Cromwell tanks of 8th King's Royal Irish Hussars rumble along with the Victory Column making a suitable background.

H. William Tetlow, Kemsley M4270X

The top brass and VIPs made their way along the line of men and equipment in a procession of half-tracks. Standing quietly in the second vehicle was Clement Attlee. He had come to Berlin awaiting the general election results from Britain. By the time the Potsdam Conference ended he was prime minister. The British electorate had rejected the Conservatives giving Labour a landslide victory with a majority of 145 seats. Churchill had led the nation to victory and survival in war, but Attlee's time had come and his administration lived up to their promises of much-needed social reform including the launch of the National Health Service.

H. William Tetlow, Kemsley M4270X

TOP LEFT The Belsen trial began on 17th September 1945 and it gave Brigadier Glyn Hughes the opportunity to describe the horrors he had seen. Transcripts of the trial do not make easy reading but they lay bare the cynical brutality of thoroughly unpleasant functionaries of the Nazi regime. Glyn Hughes was pretty much a 'total soldier' in the spirit of the times, a decorated Great War veteran with two DSOs and an MC who had turned to medicine and despite his calling found himself directing tanks during the latter stages of *Market Garden* for which he was awarded a second Bar to the DSO. He said of Belsen 'I have been a doctor for over thirty years and have seen all the horrors of war, but I have never seen anything to touch it.'

H. William Tetlow, Kemsley M4275J

BOTTOM LEFT The faces of evil: 38-year-old Haupsturmführer Josef Kramer was commandant of Belsen and had been the assistant to Rudolf Höss at Auschwitz where he was in charge of operations for six months during 1944. He began his career at Dachau in 1934. Sitting on Kramer's left is Fritz Klein, the camp doctor at Belsen. He, too, had been at Auschwitz and had taken part in the selection of victims for the gas chamber. Said Klein 'My Hippocratic oath tells me to cut out a gangrenous appendix. The Jews are the gangrenous appendix of mankind. That's why I cut them out.' Both were found guilty of crimes against humanity and hanged at Hamelin by Albert Pierrepoint on 13th December 1945.

H. William Tetlow, Kemsley M4275J

RIGHT Herta Ehlert ('8') was described at the trial as being 'sly and vicious' but escaped the death penalty and received fifteen years in prison, although she was released in 1953. The infamy of Irma Grese ('9'), just 21 years old at the time of her trial, has endured although some of her colleagues who escaped the death penalty were equally unpleasant. Her career included periods at Ravensbrück and Auschwitz before her arrival at Belsen. She acquired the name 'Beautiful Beast' during the trial where her sadistic behaviour towards inmates was recorded. She was hanged at Hamelin on 13th December 1945. Ilse Lothe ('10') was acquitted.

H. William Tetlow, Kemsley M4275J.

Often intense interest in weapons developed by the Nazis shows no sign of abating. Any difficulty understanding why the Germans lost the war given their apparent technical superiority has to be tempered with the reality that having too many designs distracted the Nazi war machine from concentrating on a smaller number of potential war winners. A display of enemy aircraft was included with a gathering of new British designs at Farnborough in October 1945. This Dornier Do335-A12 *Pfeil* (Arrow) was one of only two completed before the Americans overran the factory. The aircraft was given to the British for evaluation but was not earmarked for preservation. The A-12 variant was a tandem two-seater trainer. Eleven production examples of single-seat fighter-bombers were completed but only one survives.

Sidney Beadell, Kemsley M42780

Photographer Sidney Beadell tells us this extraordinary combination is a *Pick-a-back*. To the Germans it was a *Huckepack* although the official name for the weapon was *Beethoven*. The top-mounted Focke-Wulf Fw190 fighter would launch the un-manned Junkers Ju88 packed with explosives as a flying bomb aimed at precision targets. The Ju88 element had the official name *Mistel* (Mistletoe) and could carry just under 4,000lb of explosives. Variations of aircraft were used for the concept and at least 250 were built. Several operated against targets in Normandy following D-Day but German claims of successes do not match the Allies' version of events. The Fw190 shown here survives in the Imperial War Museum collection.

Sidney Beadell, Kemsley M4278O

The trial of leading Nazis began at Nuremberg on 20th November 1945. Bill Tetlow recorded much of the day-to-day activity in the courtroom and he found time to take behind-the-scenes images. This impressive 'join-up' is made from three negatives. Leading Nazis Hermann Göring, Rudolf Hess, Joachim von Ribbentrop and Wilhelm Keitel sit in the front row of the dock from left to right. Göring committed suicide the night before his execution. Hess would spend the rest of his life in Spandau Prison. Both von Ribbentrop and Keitel were hanged on 16th January 1946.

H. William Tetlow, Kemsley M4280Y

TOP Bill Tetlow is a picture of concentration at Nuremberg. This is one of two 35mm frames showing him at work. No other images of him remain in the News UK archive but his stunning work has been a major feature of this book.

Kemsley M4282X

BOTTOM The gifted portrait photographer Heinrich Hoffmann was imprisoned for profiteering. He had been a good friend of Adolf Hitler and became his personal photographer during the rise of the Nazis making him a very wealthy man. The Americans confiscated his vast archive and shipped it to the United States, placing his work in the public domain. Hoffmann's account of the 1940 Blitzkrieg campaign, *Mit Hitler am Westen*, and his post-war autobiography, *Hitler Was My Friend*, have recently been reprinted.

H. William Tetlow, Kemsley M4280Y

Bill Tetlow stayed on in Berlin photographing a city of contrasts as it took its place on the uneasy post-war frontier between East and West. Although much of the city was in ruins, many people were surprisingly well dressed in comparison to a dowdy London. But behind the smiles, food and fuel shortages were a cause for serious concern for Berliners as winter approached.

H. William Tetlow, Kemsley M42690 and M4278B.

TOP The European war had ended and victory over Japan was just weeks away. These young Berliners pictured by Bill Tetlow in July 1945 were certainly not the last to use abandoned weaponry as climbing frames. The News UK photographic archive has many similar examples from over half a century of conflict that followed the Second World War. Cameras and technology may have advanced beyond the imagination of the photographers featured in this book, but they would see little difference in the devastation they recorded in Caen, Arnhem and Berlin with their modern-day counterparts in the first two decades of this century.

H. William Tetlow, Kemsley M4269D

BOTTOM Although happy encounters between Brits and Russians looked good on camera, the Cold War between former partners in victory over the Nazis would dominate affairs in Europe for nearly half a century. Berlin would not be restored as the capital of a united Germany until 1990.

H William Tetlow, Kemsley M4278G

EPILOGUE

On Monday 16th March 1953, Bill Warhurst was photographing a dress rehearsal at the Shakespeare Memorial Theatre in Stratford-on-Avon when he collapsed and died. He was 56 years old. Recalling Bill two days later a colleague said of him:

> He seemed to be quite fearless. While in North-West Europe during the final campaign there he would constantly demand to be conducted, or, preferably, find his own way, to some place where 'there might be some action.' [Having] arrived in the neighbourhood of the expected (or already begun) liveliness, he would take care that his Army driver with his jeep was parked as safely as possible, then light a cigarette and go 'looking for trouble.' Bill calmly took many a picture more or less under fire on days out like that. But it was not his habit to brag of these things.

Bill Warhurst. *The Times 139632*

Selected Bibliography

Bouchury, Jean, *The Canadian Soldier*, Histoire & Collections, Paris 2003

Fortin, Ludovic, *British Tanks in Normandy*, Histoire & Collections, Paris 2005

Franks, Norman, *Ton-up Lancs*, Grub Street Publishing, London 2015

Hartwell, Keith Raymond, *Ink & Images*, Big Catz, 2008

Keegan, John, *Six Armies in Normandy*, Jonathan Cape, London 1982

Knott, Richard, *The Sketchbook War*, The History Press, Brimscombe Port, Stroud 2013

Longden, Sean, *T Force*, Constable & Robinson, London 2009

Margry, Karel, *Operation Market Garden Then and Now*, After the Battle, Hobbs Cross 2002

Mead, Richard, *The Men Behind Monty*, Pen & Sword Military, Barnsley 2015

Middlebrook, Martin & Everitt, Chris, *The Bomber Command War Diaries*, Pen & Sword Aviation, Barnsley 2014

Mortimer Moore, William, *Paris '44*, Casemate, Oxford 2015

Pallud, Jean Paul, *Rückmarsch! The German Retreat from Normandy Then and Now*, After the Battle, Hobbs Cross 2006

Ramsey, Winston G., *D-Day Then and Now*, After the Battle, London 1995

Rankin, Nicholas, *Ian Fleming's Commandos*, Faber & Faber, London 2012

Russell, John, *No Triumphant Procession*, Arms & Armour Press, London 1994

Ryan, Cornelius, *The Last Battle*, William Collins Sons & Co, London 1966

Thompson, Julian, *The Imperial War Museum Book of Victory in Europe*, Sidgwick & Jackson, London 1994